JUN 7 '00 **DATE DUE**

Demco, Inc. 38-293

WORLD
HISTORY SERIES ▪ ▪ ▪

The Age of Napoleon

Titles in the World History Series

The Age of Augustus
The Age of Feudalism
The Age of Pericles
The Alamo
America in the 1960s
The American Frontier
The American Revolution
Ancient Greece
The Ancient Near East
Architecture
Aztec Civilization
The Battle of the
  Little Bighorn
The Black Death
The Byzantine Empire
Caesar's Conquest of Gaul
The California Gold Rush
The Chinese Cultural
  Revolution
The Civil Rights Movement
The Collapse of the
  Roman Republic
The Conquest of Mexico
The Crimean War
The Crusades
The Cuban Missile Crisis
The Cuban Revolution
The Early Middle Ages
Egypt of the Pharaohs
Elizabethan England
The End of the Cold War
The French and Indian War
The French Revolution
The Glorious Revolution
The Great Depression
Greek and Roman
  Mythology
Greek and Roman Science

Greek and Roman Theater
The History of Slavery
Hitler's Reich
The Hundred Years' War
The Industrial Revolution
The Inquisition
The Italian Renaissance
The Late Middle Ages
The Lewis and Clark
  Expedition
The Mexican Revolution
The Mexican War of
  Independence
Modern Japan
The Mongol Empire
The Persian Empire
The Punic Wars
The Reformation
The Relocation of the
  North American Indian
The Renaissance
The Roaring Twenties
The Roman Empire
The Roman Republic
Roosevelt and the New Deal
The Russian Revolution
Russia of the Tsars
The Scientific Revolution
The Spread of Islam
The Stone Age
Traditional Africa
Traditional Japan
The Travels of Marco Polo
Twentieth Century Science
The Wars of the Roses
The Watts Riot
Women's Suffrage

WORLD
HISTORY SERIES ■ ■ ■

The Age of Napoleon

by Harry Henderson

Lucent Books, P.O. Box 289011, San Diego, CA 92198-9011

Library of Congress Cataloging-in-Publication Data

Henderson, Harry, 1951 Jan. 5–
    The age of Napoleon / by Harry Henderson.
        p. cm.—(World history series)
    Includes bibliographical references and index.
Summary: Discusses French history under the influence of
Napoleon Bonaparte's rise from lowly origins to military and
political power, ending with his defeat and the legacy he left to
Europe.
    ISBN 1-56006-319-X (alk. paper)
    1. Napoleon I, Emperor of the French, 1769–1821—Influ-
ence—Juvenile literature. 2. France—History—Revolution,
1789–1799—Campaigns—Juvenile literature. 3. Napoleonic
Wars, 1800–1815—Campaigns—Juvenile literature. [1.
Napoleon I, Emperor of the French, 1769–1821. 2. Kings,
queens, rulers, etc. 3. France—History—1789–1815. 4.
Napoleonic Wars, 1800–1815.] I. Title. II. Series.
DC203.9.H46   1999
944.05—dc21   98-8372
                                                              CIP
                                                               AC

Contents

Foreword

Each year on the first day of school, nearly every history teacher faces the task of explaining why his or her students should study history. One logical answer to this question is that exploring what happened in our past explains how the things we often take for granted—our customs, ideas, and institutions—came to be. As statesman and historian Winston Churchill put it, "Every nation or group of nations has its own tale to tell. Knowledge of the trials and struggles is necessary to all who would comprehend the problems, perils, challenges, and opportunities which confront us today." Thus, a study of history puts modern ideas and institutions in perspective. For example, though the founders of the United States were talented and creative thinkers, they clearly did not invent the concept of democracy. Instead, they adapted some democratic ideas that had originated in ancient Greece and with which the Romans, the British, and others had experimented. An exploration of these cultures, then, reveals their very real connection to us through institutions that continue to shape our daily lives.

Another reason often given for studying history is the idea that lessons exist in the past from which contemporary societies can benefit and learn. This idea, although controversial, has always been an intriguing one for historians. Those who agree that society can benefit from the past often quote philosopher George Santayana's famous statement, "Those who cannot remember the past are condemned to repeat it." Historians who subscribe to Santayana's philosophy believe that, for example, studying the events that led up to the major world wars or other significant historical events would allow society to chart a different and more favorable course in the future.

Just as difficult as convincing students to realize the importance of studying history is the search for useful and interesting supplementary materials that present historical events in a context that can be easily understood. The volumes in Lucent Books' World History Series attempt to present a broad, balanced, and penetrating view of the march of history. Ancient Egypt's important wars and rulers, for example, are presented against the rich and colorful backdrop of Egyptian religious, social, and cultural developments. The series engages the reader by enhancing historical events with these cultural contexts. For example, in *Ancient Greece*, the text covers the role of women in that society. Slavery is discussed in *The Roman Empire*, as well as how slaves earned their freedom. The numerous and varied aspects of everyday life in these and other societies are explored in each volume of the series. Additionally, the series covers the major political, cultural, and philosophical ideas as the torch of civilization is passed from ancient Mesopotamia and Egypt, through Greece, Rome, Medieval Europe, and other world cultures, to the modern day.

The material in the series is formatted in a thorough, precise, and organized manner. Each volume offers the reader a comprehensive and clearly written overview of an important historical event or period. The topic under discussion is placed in a broad historical context. For example, *The Italian Renaissance* begins with a discussion of the High Middle Ages and the loss of central control that allowed certain Italian cities to develop artistically. The book ends by looking forward to the Reformation and interpreting the societal changes that grew out of the Renaissance. Thus, students are not only involved in an historical era, but also enveloped by the events leading up to that era and the events following it.

One important and unique feature in the World History Series is the primary and secondary source quotations that richly supplement each volume. These quotes are useful in a number of ways. First, they allow students access to sources they would not normally be exposed to because of the difficulty and obscurity of the original source. The quotations range from interesting anecdotes to farsighted cultural perspectives and are drawn from historical witnesses both past and present. Second, the quotes demonstrate how and where historians themselves derive their information on the past as they strive to reach a consensus on historical events. Lastly, all of the

quotes are footnoted, familiarizing students with the citation process and allowing them to verify quotes and/or look up the original source if the quote piques their interest.

Finally, the books in the World History Series provide a detailed launching point for further research. Each book contains a bibliography specifically geared toward student research. A second, annotated bibliography introduces students to all the sources the author consulted when compiling the book. A chronology of important dates gives students an overview, at a glance, of the topic covered. Where applicable, a glossary of terms is included.

In short, the series is designed not only to acquaint readers with the basics of history, but also to make them aware that their lives are a part of an ongoing human saga. Perhaps they will then come to the same realization as famed historian Arnold Toynbee. In his monumental work, *A Study of History*, he wrote about becoming aware of history flowing through him in a mighty current, and of his own life "welling like a wave in the flow of this vast tide."

Important Dates in the Age of Napoleon

1789	1792	1793	1794	1795	1796	1797	1798	1799	1800	18

1789
July 14—Storming of the Bastille ignites the French Revolution.

1792
French Republic goes to war with Prussia and Austria; French beat Prussians at Valmy and Austrians at Jemappes.

1793
January—King Louis XVI beheaded; Reign of Terror begins; about twenty-five thousand people executed as enemies of the Republic.

December—Napoleon drives British naval forces away from Toulon.

1794
July—Overthrow of Robespierre ends Reign of Terror; conservative forces gain strength.

August—Napoleon temporarily arrested because of association with Robespierre.

1795
October 5—Napoleon's cannons put down Paris revolt.

November 3—Directory government established.

1796
March 9—Napoleon marries Joséphine de Beauharnais, then begins Italian campaign.

May 10—Napoleon wins battle at Lodi.

November 15–18—Napoleon wins at Arcola.

1797
January—Napoleon wins battle at Rivoli Veronese.

October 18—Treaty of Campo Formio confirms French control in northern Italy and establishment of French satellite republics.

1798
May—Napoleon begins Egyptian campaign.

July 21—Napoleon wins Battle of the Pyramids.

July 31—British admiral Horatio Nelson destroys Napoleon's fleet in Battle of the Nile at Abukir Bay.

1799
March–June—Napoleon marches toward Syria but is eventually forced to retreat to Egypt.

October—Napoleon returns to France, and rumors of a coup lead to his takeover as First Consul; meanwhile, Austrians regain much of Italy.

1800
May—Napoleon invades Italy through the Great St. Bernard pass.

June 14—Battle of Marengo completes Napoleon's reconquest of Italy.

1802
March 27—French Revolutionary War ends with Treaty of Amiens between France and Britain.

April 8—Agreement with the pope restores limited rights for the Catholic Church in France.

August 2—Napoleon becomes consul for life.

1803
May—Napoleonic Wars begin as Britain and France block each other's trade; Napoleon sells Louisiana to United States.

1804
March 21—Napoleonic Code introduced.

December 2—Napoleon crowned emperor of France.

1805
October—Napoleon surrounds and captures Austrian general Karl Mack's forces at Ulm.

October 21—Nelson destroys French-Spanish fleet at Trafalgar, ending plans to invade Britain.

December 3—Napoleon wins decisive victory against Austrians and Russians at Austerlitz.

1806
July 12—Napoleon creates Confederation of the Rhine to replace Holy Roman Empire.

October 14—Napoleon defeats Prussians at Jena.

November—Napoleon invades Poland in an attempt to dislodge Russian influence.

November 21—Napoleon declares "Continental System," European trade boycott against Britain.

November 28—Napoleon captures Warsaw but is unable to catch retreating Russians.

1807
February 8—Bloody but indecisive Battle of Eylau fought in terrible winter weather.

June 14—French victory at Friedland leads to Russia being forced to join the Continental System in Treaty of Tilsit.

October 27—French troops enter Spain to attack Portugal.

1808
May 2—Spanish citizens revolt against Napoleon's takeover of Spanish monarchy; later in the year, Napoleon sends reinforcements to Spain; British general Arthur Wellesley, duke of Wellington, fights successful defensive battles.

1809
May 21–22—Napoleon suffers major military setbacks at Aspern and Essling; conflict arises between Napoleon and Czar Alexander of Russia when Napoleon marries Marie–Louise of Austria, having had his marriage to Joséphine annulled; Russia abandons the Continental System.

1811
The duke of Wellington takes the offensive in Spain as guerillas harass French troops.

1812
June—Napoleon invades Russia.

September 7—Napoleon and Russian general Mikhail Kutuzov fight indecisive battle at Borondino.

September 14—French enter Moscow, but the city is deserted.

October 19—French begin long retreat from Russia; many perish from cold, disease, and starvation.

1813
French virtually driven out of Spain.

October 16–18—Napoleon defeated at the Battle of the Nations in Leipzig; loses control of his empire.

1814
April 11—Napoleon abdicates the throne and is exiled to Elba; the Congress of Vienna begins to restore the old monarchies and establishes a balance of power in Europe.

1815
February 26—Napoleon escapes from Elba.

March 20—Napoleon reaches Paris and rebuilds army to invade Belgium; the "Hundred Days" begins.

June 16—Napoleon defeats Prussians at Quatre Bras but fails to deliver the knockout blow.

June 18—Napoleon decisively defeated by the duke of Wellington and Marshal Gebhard von Blücher at Waterloo.

July 15—Napoleon is exiled on St. Helena, where he dies on May 5, 1821.

The Birth of the Modern

In his great novel *War and Peace*, Russian novelist Leo Tolstoy sets the stage for the Age of Napoleon, a brief but profoundly important time in European history:

> The first fifteen years of the nineteenth century present the spectacle of an extraordinary movement of millions of men. Men leave their habitual pursuits; rush from one side of Europe to another; plunder, slaughter one another, triumph and despair; and the whole current of life is transformed. . . . What was the cause of that activity, or from what laws did it rise?[1]

For the past two centuries, historians have continued to seek explanations for the Napoleonic Wars, a string of conflicts that killed about four million soldiers and civilians between 1798 and 1815. No nation in Europe—indeed, no city or village—would be untouched by loss of life and economic hardships caused by the first true "world war." The conflict would spread overseas, bringing opportunities and challenges to both the United States and Latin America.

In many ways Europe around 1800 was on the brink of the modern world. As the Industrial Revolution gained momentum, a growing network of industry and colonial trade had begun to make nations more de-

pendant on one another. Increasingly, it was the manufacturers and the merchants who were most important for the success of a nation. Yet the social fabric was still being held together by feudalism, an inflexible system of mutual obligations that bound kings and their nobles to each other and to the peasant farmers, to the extreme disadvantage of the poor. But developing in this centuries-old society was a new middle class, called the bourgeoisie, consisting of nonagricultural workers, tradespeople, and other city dwellers.

A Time of Change

The negative effects of feudalism, coupled with the rising demands of the bourgeoisie for representation in government, produced immense strains; when the fabric of the old European order gave way, it was in France that the first tear appeared. Thus a revolution began in Paris in 1789 that soon threatened the rule of kings throughout Europe.

The new forms of government and social organization pioneered by the French republic made it possible to mobilize an entire nation. Awakening nationalism motivated newly empowered citizens to seek glory. The result was the forerunner of the modern national army. These new armies, which became the main instruments of national policy, dwarfed the forces of medieval kings and Renaissance princes. Such instruments, moreover, were built to be used. Thus, even in the absence of truly extraordinary individuals, it is likely that numerous local wars and conflicts would have occurred as national interests clashed.

Enter Napoleon

But into this extraordinary time was injected an extraordinary young man named Napoleon Bonaparte. Napoleon had intelligence, aggressiveness, and ambition, and he used these characteristics to harness the emerging forces of nationalism and build Europe's greatest empire since Roman times. As the peoples of Italy, Germany, Spain, Russia, and other countries encountered Napoleon's power, they began to discover their own national identities. They began to fight Napoleon with his own tactics and ideas. Again and again, European rulers joined together to defeat Napoleon. When they succeeded they were obliged to reconcile their desire to return to the old order—the rule of kings—with the demands and emerging

Political prisoners are liberated from Paris's mighty penitentiary, the Bastille, during the French Revolution. The Revolution would reshape the nation and inspire patriotism among its citizenry.

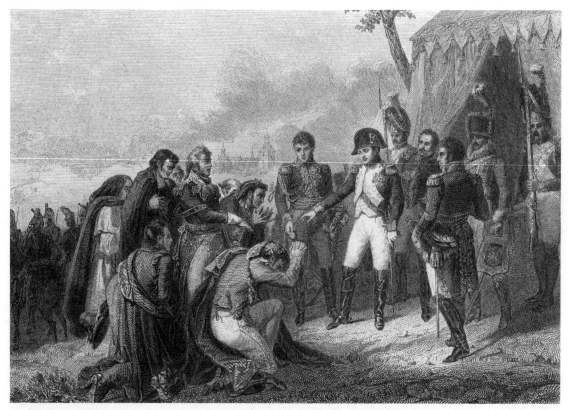

An ambitious Napoleon Bonaparte prepares to seize Madrid, Spain, despite the pleas of the city's residents who have gathered before the mighty general.

power of the middle class, of trade and industry, and of working people.

The story of Napoleon and his times engages our human interest in a leader who was paradoxical, fascinating, controversial, and larger-than-life. Here was a man who declared himself to be the fulfillment of a revolution for liberty, yet he would crown himself an emperor of absolute power. Here was a general who could analyze an enemy position and then crush it with carefully timed blows, yet he was slow to understand that wars could be fought without battles. Here was a ruler who rearranged conquered nations like pieces in a giant puzzle that in the end he could not solve.

In considering Napoleon's empire and its impact on Europe, we see the beginnings of the great nations and powers that would shape much of world history during the twentieth century.

1 Seizing the Day: Napoleon's Revolutionary Opportunity

In the hours after midnight on December 19, 1793, the skies over the southern French port of Toulon were lit as bright as day. Ten battleships blazed fiercely, sending up vast clouds of black smoke. On shore, explosions thundered as fires consumed ammunition stockpiles. The ships had been torched by their own crews, a time-honored tactic used by defeated navies to keep valuable vessels out of enemy hands. The remaining ships were hastily put to sea, as crews chose evacuation over certain defeat.

It would be hard to determine what was most remarkable about this scene. Perhaps it was that the evacuees represented kings throughout Europe—kings who were no longer fighting among themselves but had joined forces to invade a country that threatened kingship itself. Or, perhaps it was the young artillery officer named Napoleon Bonaparte who had planned the attack on the ships. He had begun a career that would lead the French republic to victory after victory, while transforming it into a superpower and a dictatorship that changed the face of Europe.

The Fire of Revolution

Society in the Middle Ages was rigidly divided into classes. At the top were kings, who claimed their right to rule stemmed from God. Below kings were the regional nobles, whose positions were ensured at birth. The clergy occupied a separate hierarchy headed by the pope, whom the kings considered to be a fellow ruler having the added prestige of being God's representative on Earth. And at the bottom were the common people, who had little hope of rising above their parents' (and grandparents') station in life.

With this apparently stable arrangement, what had caused kings to become endangered species? The causes of the French Revolution are complex, and historians have argued for generations about their significance; but the spark of the Revolution was surely new ideas. Starting about a century earlier, social thinkers such as John Locke in England, followed by Jean-Jacques Rousseau and Baron Montesquieu in France, had developed new theories of government based on a "scientific," rational approach.

Rather than automatically accepting the idea that kings ruled by divine right, the new thinkers saw government as a tool created by human beings to serve human needs and indeed to protect people's rights. A hallmark of this reason-based philosophical movement, called the Enlightenment, was the belief in fundamental human rights.

English philosopher John Locke (pictured) and other social thinkers of the Enlightenment supported fundamental human rights and questioned the power of the government.

In 1776 Thomas Jefferson's Declaration of Independence had boldly stated these ideas as the basis for an independent American republic. Ironically, the French monarchy had supported the American Revolution with considerable money, supplies, and military forces. This support reflected both sympathy for the new ideas of liberty and a desire to weaken Great Britain, France's rival for domination of North America earlier in the century. But the expenditures for aid, plus the borrowing needed to support the lavish lifestyle of the French royal court, had brought France close to bankruptcy. While the government's corrupt tax collectors lined their pockets, prices soared and workers found their wages lagging far behind. To pay off the national debt, King Louis XVI demanded a tax increase, but the nobles, whose consent was required, refused to go along with the measure.

Instead, the nobles issued their own demand, calling on the king to assemble the Estates General, an ancient but seldom-used congress. In this three-part body, the First Estate consisted of the clergy (bishops and priests), while the Second Estate was made up of the nobles. The Third Estate consisted of the remaining 98 percent of the population who were the growing middle class in the cities, the workers, and the peasants across the countryside.

The nobles and clergy were exempt from most taxes, so the burden fell almost completely on the Third Estate, particularly peasants and workers. According to the traditional rules of the Estates General, however, each of the three estates collectively cast a single vote. This meant that the nobles and clergy could overrule the much more numerous Third Estate and impose taxes on the latter.

Under these conditions merchants, manufacturers, and the growing urban middle class grew dissatisfied with their lack of political power. They would find their voice in a pamphlet entited "What Is the Third Estate?" The pamphlet's author, a clergyman named Emmanuel-Joseph Sieyès, bluntly answered his own question: "Everything. What has it been till now? Nothing. What does it want to be? Something, or . . . everything."[2]

Prompted by this radical viewpoint, the representatives of the Third Estate demanded that the voting rules be changed to give each delegate, rather than each estate, a vote. When this attempt to overcome the automatic majority of the nobles and clergy was denied, the Third Estate declared itself to be the National Assembly, the representatives of all the French people. Some members of the first two estates joined the assembly. Weak and indecisive, Louis XVI wavered, seeming to agree with the new arrangement one moment, while ordering up troops the next.

To make matters worse, harvests had been bad and a grain shortage and high bread prices threatened many people with starvation. Many workers and tradespeople in Paris began to gather weapons. On July 14, 1789, they stormed the Bastille, an ancient and forbidding prison fortress, slaughtering guards and freeing political prisoners. "Why that is a revolt!" exclaimed the astonished king. "No, Sire," one noble replied, "it is a revolution!"[3] But the real revolution had occurred when the Third Estate had attempted to institute a simple form of popular government; this action implied that the people, not the king, were the ultimate source of authority. The question was now whether French society could be peacefully transformed.

From Reform to Revolution

The National Assembly, which the king had reluctantly authorized, began to design a new government by issuing the Declaration of the Rights of Man and of the Citizen.

This famous document identifies the rights of individual liberty, political participation, and equal treatment of citizens,

Brandishing weapons, angry French citizens storm the Bastille on July 14, 1789, setting the French Revolution in motion.

and it is quite similar to the U.S. Constitution's Bill of Rights. With the Declaration as their cornerstone, French legislators began to draft their own constitution, specifying how government would be organized and how power would be shared.

At first most legislators favored a constitutional monarchy, wherein the king would remain as the head of the government but decisions about taxes, laws, and foreign policy would require the approval of the legislature. (This system had been used in Great Britain since the 1660s.)

King Louis XVI debated whether he should agree to be a constitutional monarch or whether he should seek the help of other European kings to restore an absolute monarchy. The National Assembly struggled with social chaos and economic breakdown. Mobs of peasants attacked nobles, burning their manor houses and forcing them to flee the country.

A "Bill of Rights" for the French People

The French Declaration of the Rights of Man and of the Citizen, similar in many ways to the Bill of Rights in the U.S. Constitution, also echoes the Preamble to the Constitution and the Declaration of Independence. The following excerpts highlight the similarities between the documents.

"Article 1. Men are born and remain free and equal in rights. . . .

Article 2. The aim of all political association is the natural and [nonremovable] rights of man. These rights are liberty, property, security, and resistance to oppression. . . .

Article 4. Liberty consists in the freedom to do everything which injures no one else. . . .

Article 6. Law is the expression of the general will. Every citizen has a right to participate personally, or through his representative, in its formation. . . . All citizens, being equal in the eyes of the law, are equally eligible to all dignities and to all public positions and occupations, according to their abilities. . . .

Article 7. No person shall be accused, arrested, or imprisoned except in the cases, and according to the forms, prescribed by law.

Article 11. The free communication of ideas and opinions is one of the most precious of the rights of man. Every citizen, may, accordingly, speak, write, and print with freedom, but shall be responsible for such abuses of this freedom as shall be defined by law."

While French peasants rally together, a child curiously looks at the body of a dead revolutionist. Poor harvests, grain shortages, and soaring bread prices forced many peasants to the brink of starvation.

Perhaps some had initially hoped that the French Revolution would run its course like the uprising in America, with deaths confined largely to armed combatants and relatively little disruption of business in Europe. But America was far away from England and from the aged, nearly dysfunctional monarchies of the continent. Thus, liberties won by colonists across the Atlantic did not threaten the balance of power in Europe. A revolution in the very heart of Europe was a different matter.

In France, the more radical revolutionaries wanted to get rid of the monarchy completely. In effect, they declared war against kingship—not only in France but also abroad. According to historian David Chandler, "They would create 'one great

revolution'; it would become 'a crusade for universal liberty.'" Their cry was "We shall live in freedom or we shall die!"[4] Revolutionary fervor about the birth of a new nation was intertwined with a surge of nationalism: It was "special" to be part of this hopeful new society. "The French have become the foremost people in the universe,"[5] one writer exulted. The constitution adopted by the National Assembly in 1791 was more moderate, but it created a legislature and defined the limits of the king's power. Louis XVI, again reluctantly, accepted the new governing charter.

Not surprisingly, monarchs in Austria, Prussia, the German states, Britain, and elsewhere were alarmed at the possibility that the French Revolution would spill over

French nationalists attack the Tuileries palace in Paris, inciting the legislature to abolish the monarchy in favor of a republic.

threats from well-armed royalist neighbors spurred French nationalism and helped the radicals take control of the legislature.

The duke of Brunswick's eighty thousand Prussian, Austrian, and other troops invaded France, driving the hastily assembled French army back toward Paris. As Brunswick's troops approached the city, the duke announced that

> the city of Paris and all its inhabitants shall be required to submit at once and without delay to the King. . . . Their Majesties declare . . . that if the Chateau of the Tuileries is entered by force or attacked, if the least violence be offered to . . . the King, the Queen, and the royal family, and if their safety and liberty be not immediately assured, they will inflict an ever memorable vengeance by delivering over the city of Paris to military execution and complete destruction.[6]

In response, an angry mob stormed the Tuileries palace, and the king was locked up for his own protection. The legislature called another round of elections to choose representatives for a convention that would replace the constitutional monarchy with a kingless republic. These measures were quickly put into effect, and in less than two months the new convention had abolished the monarchy and declared the First French Republic.

The Embattled Republic

The army of the revolutionary republic combined a considerable number of experienced soldiers who had belonged to the royal army and a growing swarm of new re-

the borders into surrounding countries. In August 1791 émigrés (French nobles who had fled the mob violence) convinced Austria and Prussia to issue the Declaration of Pillnitz, which made its goal the complete restoration of the French monarchy by force. In turn, the French Assembly declared war against the emperor of Austria in April 1792. By signing the Pillnitz accord, Austria and Prussia had in effect formed a coalition against France; it was the first of seven such alliances among various European powers during the Age of Napoleon. The two German-speaking countries were joined by Great Britain in 1793. These

cruits. What the new recruits lacked in experience they made up in motivation. While their opponents fought because they had been ordered to support their kings in causes that often meant little to the common soldier, the French revolutionaries believed they were fighting for their freedom and the future of their country. As Napoleon would later note,

> the French soldier is not a machine to be put in motion but a reasonable being that must be directed. . . . [He] loves to argue, because he is intelligent. . . . When he approves of the operations and respects his superiors, there is nothing he cannot do.[7]

During the eighteenth century, professional armies normally fought standing shoulder-to-shoulder in lines that stretched across the battlefield. This formation allowed for maximum firepower since all muskets could be brought to bear at once. But keeping the lines straight, let alone maneuvering them, required skill and practice. The French did not have the time to drill their new recruits to fight this way, so instead they often sent them across the battlefield in narrow columns many men deep. While columns were at a disadvantage in firepower, they could move quickly and sometimes surprise and overwhelm the enemy's more cumbersome lines.

High morale, improvised tactics, and good defensive strategy helped the French delay the invaders. Finally, using the barrier of the Argonne Forest at Valmy and superior gunnery, French forces under Charles-François Dumouriez and François-Christophe de Kellermann stopped the invaders, who fled back toward Germany, fighting disease as well as the triumphant French. In another decisive clash, Dumouriez defeated an Austrian force under Archduke Albert near the town of Jemappes in Belgium. The republic had been saved, but its nature would soon change irrevocably.

The year 1793 began with King Louis's head rolling from the guillotine and Britain and France going to war. The French National Convention declared that,

> from now until such time as its enemies have been driven out of the territory of the republic, all Frenchmen are permanently requisitioned for the service of the armies. The young shall go and fight, the married men shall forge weapons and transport food, the women shall make tents and clothes and serve in the hospitals, the old men shall have themselves carried into public places to rouse the courage of the warriors and preach hatred of kings and the unity of the nation.[8]

France would become "a nation in arms."

Napoleon of Corsica

It often seems that the people who have most changed the destiny of nations have come from outside their borders. For example, Adolf Hitler was an Austrian, not a German; Joseph Stalin was a Georgian, not a Russian; and the ancient conqueror Alexander the Great had been Macedonian, not Greek. Napoleon fits in this pattern: He was born (with the name Nabulio) in Corsica on August 15, 1769.

Corsica is an island in the Mediterranean Sea located off the west coast of Italy, just north of the larger Sardinia. It had been ruled by the Italian city-state of Genoa since the fourteenth century. The year before Napoleon's birth, however, Genoa sold the island to France (without, of course, consulting its inhabitants.)

Corsica had been described by the ancient Roman writer Livy as "a rugged, mountainous, almost uninhabitable island. The people resemble their country, being as ungovernable as wild beasts."[9] Despite Livy's harsh assessment, over the centuries the Corsican nobles and educated class had adopted Italian culture and some

were now open to the ideas of the Enlightenment that had rocked France. But the common people retained their strong family ties as they struggled with poverty, fought feuds among themselves, and resisted invaders. Napoleon's parents had followed the anti-Genoese forces of Pasquale Paoli through the mountains, and Napoleon grew up with that tradition of resistance always before his eyes.

While the French repressed Corsican nationalism, they also brought new opportunities to the Corsican nobility as they

The end of the monarchy foreshadowed the end of the indecisive King Louis XVI. In 1793, before a crowd that had gathered to witness his execution, Louis was beheaded by the guillotine.

tried to create a sympathetic educated class that would bring reform and "enlightened" rule to the island. When Paoli's rebellion failed, Napoleon's father, Carlo, made peace with the French and received a scholarship to send Napoleon and his brother Joseph to the royal military school in Brienne-le-Château, France.

"Aspiring to Everything"

Napoleon's first language was Italian. As a boy he spoke only limited French, and his strong Corsican accent was ridiculed by his classmates. The young Napoleon fiercely fought back, arguing for the superiority of Corsicans and denouncing the oppressiveness of the French. Biographer Alan Schom recalls how

> on one occasion [Napoleon] was disciplined by a master for disobedience and ordered to replace his uniform with rough clothing and then to eat dinner kneeling on the floor of the refectory with 109 smirking schoolboys looking on. Napoleon rebelled. "In my family we kneel only before God!" He stood there adamantly, then suddenly turned livid, seized by a violent attack that left him trembling, out of control, and vomiting. The school's superior rescinded the punishment, and a feverish Napoleon was taken back to his dormitory.[10]

Despite Napoleon's rebelliousness, his teachers soon realized that he was an intelligent, eager student:

> Reserved and studious, [Napoleon] prefers studying to any kind of amusement. He enjoys reading good authors

Corsican Napoleon Bonaparte, pictured here at age twenty-seven, would rise to great power in France, ultimately becoming the nation's emperor.

> and applies himself very well to the abstract sciences only, with a solid knowledge of mathematics and geography. He is quiet and solitary, capricious, haughty, and frightfully egotistical. He replies energetically to questions in class and is swift and sharp in his repartee at other times. He is most proud, ambitious, aspiring to everything. This young man merits our consideration and help.[11]

Napoleon's reading exposed him to many exciting ideas. He certainly would have read about the great ancient generals such as Hannibal, Julius Caesar, and Alexander the Great. Perhaps he had daydreams of campaigns of conquest. He also encountered "modern" ideas of political philosophy, including Rousseau's theory of social rights. Exposure to an array of views about good government helped prepare Napoleon for his future as a ruler and a lawmaker. He also took pleasure in reading romantic and heroic literature such as epic poems about the Irish hero Ossian.

Liberty and Violence

In 1785 Napoleon was selected for advanced military training and was commissioned as second lieutenant of artillery for a regiment. The easy pace of the French military allowed plenty of time for reading, going to plays, discovering women, and pondering the meaning of life. When the French Revolution began in 1789, the young officer followed events avidly, responding to France's struggle for liberty and appealing to it on behalf of his homeland:

> How is it possible that an enlightened nation like France is not touched by our [Corsica's] plight, a direct result of their actions? . . . In the eyes of God, the worst crime is to tyrannize over men, but the next worse is to suffer such tyranny! Mankind! Mankind! How wretched you are in the state of bondage, but how great when you are impassioned by the flame of liberty![12]

Napoleon rejoiced when Corsica became a department of France in 1791, granting full rights and legal protection to all Corsicans. For Napoleon, his past seemed to be reconciled to the hopeful, exciting future of the new republic.

But the era of mob violence soon filled him with misgivings. He witnessed the mob attack on the Tuileries that had ended with the imprisonment of King Louis XVI and Queen Marie-Antoinette.

During radical Maximilien Robespierre's year-long Reign of Terror, his Committee of Public Safety persecuted anyone suspected of being a royalist.

Then, as royalists continued to plot to restore the throne and Austria, Prussia, and Britain sent their invading forces, the time called the Terror began in 1793. Under the leadership of the fanatical Maximilien Robespierre, radicals decided to purge the government—and the nation—of anyone who might work against the interests of the republic. Robespierre's Committee of Public Safety essentially took over government from the legislature and directed the arrest of people ranging from actual royalist plotters to priests, former nobles, moderates (Girondins), and anyone critical of the government. Special courts, called Revolutionary Tribunals, processed the prisoners through hasty trials in which they had little opportunity to defend themselves. By the time the Terror had burnt out in the latter half of 1794, more than twenty-five thousand people had lost their heads to that "modern" technological marvel, the guillotine.

The Cannons Speak

As the Revolution boiled over, Napoleon had been a distant observer. Back in Corsica, he joined a French military expedition against Sardinia that was sabotaged by Paoli's Corsican nationalists. By now, however, Napoleon's allegiance was to the French republic; when he denounced the Paoli faction, he found himself driven out of Corsica.

In December 1793, Napoleon was assigned as captain of artillery to the French forces besieging the port of Toulon, which was held by royalists supported by a powerful British battle fleet. The demoralized republican forces that surrounded the city had only a few cannon and little ammunition. Napoleon immediately rode out to the surrounding towns, including Avignon, Nice, and Marseilles, and scrounged up enough artillery, wagons, and ammunition to equip thirteen batteries totaling ninety guns. By carefully placing the cannon in each battery, Napoleon was able to bombard and destroy many of the British guns while harassing the ships.

When the all-out assault was finally ready, Napoleon's cannon bombarded the key forts, and troops led by Generals Dugommier and Masséna overran the royalist positions. Once the forts were taken, their guns could be turned around to fire on the British ships, so the latter had no choice but to flee.

A jailer reads a list of prisoners who are to be sent to the guillotine. More than twenty-five thousand French citizens were executed during the Terror in a misguided attempt to protect the interests of the republic.

Revolutionary Terror

In The Age of Napoleon, *J. Christopher Herold describes how the victorious republicans imposed "revolutionary justice" on the people of Toulon, many of whom had collaborated with the royalists and the British in 1793.*

"Then legality, in the shape of a revolutionary tribunal and the guillotine, took over. 'There is a high incidence of mortality among the subjects of Louis XVI,' wrote the People's Representative Fréron in a humorous vein. After one of the mass executions by musket fire, someone cried: 'Let all the wounded stand up, the Republic will pardon them!' A number of wounded managed to rise and were shot down. A man ninety-four years old was carried to the guillotine in a chair. 'All goes well here,' Fréron reported to Paris. 'We have requisitioned [drafted] 1,200 masons to demolish and raze the city. Every day since our entry we have had two hundred heads cut off.'"

In Paris, townspeople suspected of collaborating with royalists are carried to their executions. Royalists and sympathizers were brutalized as the new regime took control.

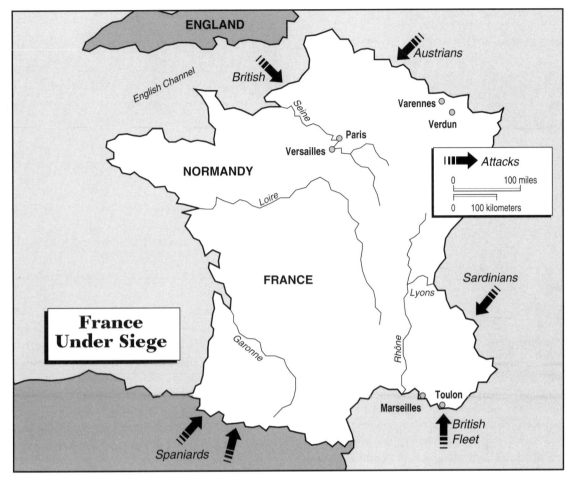

France Under Siege

The "liberation" of Toulon soon gave Napoleon his first experience as a perpetrator of revolutionary violence. Hundreds of citizens who had collaborated with the local royalists and their British supporters were rounded up in the public square. Under government orders, Napoleon's cannons blasted again, killing hundreds of them. The guillotine then finished the job.

In a letter to his brother Lucien, Napoleon wrote:

Among so many conflicting ideas and so many perspectives, the honest man is confused and distressed and the skeptic becomes wicked. Since one must take sides, one might as well choose the side that is victorious, the side which devastates, loots, and burns. Considering the alternative, it is better to eat than to be eaten.[13]

Despite any misgiving he might have had, Napoleon's career seemed promising. He was promoted to brigadier general, and he had come to the attention of the highest officials of the military. General du Teil lauded Napoleon in a letter to the French war minister:

I cannot find praiseworthy enough words to describe Bonaparte's full

Napoleon takes an enemy general prisoner during the 1793 siege of Toulon. During the so-called liberation, Napoleon and his soldiers mercilessly plundered the city.

worth. He has a solid scientific knowledge of his profession and as much intelligence, if too much courage, voilà there you have but a scant sketch of the virtues of this rare officer. It only remains for you, Minister, to consecrate his talents to the glory of the Republic![14]

On July 27, 1794, Robespierre and his governing faction were overthrown. Tired of the radical ideologues and the Terror, moderate politicians representing the bourgeoisie regained control of the legislature.

By the next year, this faction had written another constitution, one that set up yet another form of republic. Beginning in November, power would be shared by a five-man group called the Directory as well as a pair of legislative bodies. Since only members of the property-owning class would be allowed to vote, both the radical republicans and the royalists were left out in the cold. So, for a while, was Napoleon, who had been associated with Robespierre. Arrested in August and nearly tried as a terrorist, Napoleon was soon released from custody after a fellow Corsican, Antoine Saliceti, intervened on his behalf.

In October 1795 Napoleon had been working in a government topographical (map-making) office and spending his evenings enjoying the theaters and high society of Paris. While at the theater one night, he was informed that a coup d'état, or sudden takeover of the government, by a group of royalists was in progress. Some members of the Committee of Public Safety quickly persuaded Napoleon to take charge of the military garrison and organize a defense.

The next morning, October 5, two columns of royalist rebels began marching on the new government, which had installed itself grandly in offices at the Tuileries. But Napoleon was waiting, his cannon loaded with containers of buckshot-sized lead balls. As the royalists approached, the gunners opened fire. The cannons acted like huge shotguns, spraying the marchers and resulting in more than five hundred casualties. But the republic, it seemed, had been saved again. A few months later Napoleon received his reward. He was appointed commander in chief of the French army in Italy.

2 Learning His Craft: Napoleon in Italy and Egypt

Before going to his new post in Italy, Napoleon fell in love with Marie-Joséphe-Rose Tascher de la Pagerie, whose husband, Alexandre, vicomte de Beauharnais, had lost his head in the Terror. She had survived by having affairs with several well-connected officials. At one of her salons, or gatherings that featured elegance and witty conversation, Napoleon saw her and quickly fell in love. Addressing her as "Joséphine," Napoleon waged an insistent campaign for her hand and married her on March 9, 1796. Their courtship and stormy marriage would become one of the world's great romances.

The Plains of Italy

Napoleon may have made a name for himself in Toulon and in Paris, but he would have to prove himself in Italy. While government officials focused on their political survival, the army in Italy had deteriorated both physically and mentally. The arrival of an inexperienced, politically connected general from Paris would be unlikely to impress the soldiers. As J. Christopher Herold observes,

one might expect that the arrival of a general twenty-six years old, five feet

Defeated on the Home Front

In The Age of Napoleon, *Will and Ariel Durant describe how Napoleon and Joséphine's marriage encountered its first crisis—one worthy of a modern TV sitcom.*

"They spent their wedding night at her home. He encountered virile opposition from her pet dog, Fortuné. 'That gentleman,' he tells us, 'was in possession of Madame's bed. . . . I wanted to have him leave, but to no avail; I was told to share the bed with him or sleep elsewhere; I had to take it or leave it. The favorite was less accommodating than I was. . . .' At the worst possible moment the dog bit his leg, so severely that he long kept the scar."

two inches tall, whose most decisive feat of arms had been the massacre of a few hundred civilians in the Rue St. Honoré [Paris street where the royalists had been gunned down], would do little to stir the enthusiasm of either the troops or the staff officers.[15]

But Napoleon's eyes and commanding voice more than compensated for his short stature. He quickly gained his soldiers' attention by announcing his plans:

Soldiers! You are hungry and naked; the government owes you much, but can give you nothing. Your patience and courage, displayed among these rocks, are admirable, but that brings

The elegant Joséphine became Napoleon's wife on March 9, 1796. The couple's tempestuous marriage would be marred by infidelities.

you no glory. . . . I will lead you into the most fertile plains on earth. Rich provinces, wealthy cities, all will be at your disposal; there you will find honor, glory, and riches.[16]

The promise of glory and loot motivated the army of ragged, bored soldiers. They faced a formidable challenge, however. At the end of the eighteenth century, Italy was a patchwork of states rather than a united nation. Some of these states, such as Venice and Genoa, had been powerful city-states and showplaces of the Renaissance three centuries earlier. Now, however, most of the northern plains of Italy were ruled directly or indirectly by the Habsburg Empire of Austria.

The Directory that ruled France had decided to mount a major offensive in northern Italy. It hoped to drive the Austrians out of that area, gaining influence (and loot). Meanwhile, the attack might force the Austrians to divert troops from the French border, making a new invasion of France less likely.

Napoleon's forces thrust into the island kingdom of Sardinia, northwest of the Italian mainland. An Austrian army under General Jean Beaulieu and an allied Piedmontese army under Baron Colli reacted quickly, but the two generals had problems coordinating their movements in the mountainous terrain. At first Napoleon also had problems with his subordinate generals (including Masséna, who won a battle only to be caught the very next morning). Napoleon gained control of the situation, however, and pushed his way through the hills to the Piedmont plain. He then drove his fast-moving force between the two enemy armies, pushing them apart as he attacked and defeated

A New Kind of Army

In The Napoleonic Sourcebook *military historian Philip J. Haythornthwaite points out that Napoleon had given his armies new capabilities that could not be matched by his foes.*

"In the wider context of strategy, one characteristic appears in almost all Napoleon's campaigns: the ability to contend with more than one enemy force at once, and to defeat much larger opponents by interposing his own army between the component parts of their forces, holding one enemy wing with a minority of his force and falling upon the other wing with the bulk of his army, thus achieving numerical 'local superiority' and defeating the enemy in detail. The existence of French [army corps] capable of sustaining an action independent of support, and the rapid speed of maneuver attainable by the French over short distances, made this strategy possible."

Beaulieu. He then turned on Colli's army, smashing it at Mondovì and forcing it to withdraw from the war.

This tactical approach of driving between, dividing, and separately attacking enemy armies would be used successfully by Napoleon in many future campaigns. Napoleon understood better than most of his opponents that if a general had well-motivated troops and acted decisively, he could defeat larger but slower and less well-coordinated forces.

By the end of April 1796 the satisfied Napoleon, looking toward the snow-covered Alps, remarked that "Hannibal had to climb over them; we merely walked around them."[17] He was now able to seize the supplies, ammunition, and horses that he needed to replenish his army and to satisfy his soldiers. Finally, he was able to sign an armistice with the king of Sardinia that broke that kingdom away from Austria and made it a French base of operations.

In May Napoleon quickly attacked before the Austrians could bring up reinforcements. The rapid series of victories had changed the army's morale immensely, helping to propel it forward. As historians Will and Ariel Durant observe,

in those battles the young commander impressed his subordinates with his keen and quick perception of developments, needs, and opportunities, his clear and decisive orders, the logic and success of tactics completing the foresight of strategy that often caught the enemy on flank or rear. The older generation learned to obey him with confidence in his vision and judgment; the younger officers . . . developed for him a devotion that repeatedly faced death in his cause. When, after these victories, the exhausted survivors reached the heights of Mount Zemoto—from which they could view the sunlit plains of

Lombardy—many of them broke out in a spontaneous salute to the youth who had led them so brilliantly.[18]

And as Napoleon wrote to his superiors back in Paris, the army was now totally different from the ragtag force he had met only a few months earlier:

Nothing equals the soldiers' courage unless it is the cheerfulness with which they bear up under the most exhausting marches. They sing in turn of fatherland and of love. You would think at least that on reaching the bivouac [camp] they would want to sleep. Nothing of the sort. Everybody tells of what he has done, or else talks about the next day's plan of operations, and often I find that they grasp things very clearly.[19]

The decisive battle of the early campaign came on May 10 at the town of Lodi, where Beaulieu's forces had left a strong rear guard to delay the French pursuit. As French cannons fired across the river Adda, the French troops crossed and drove the Austrians back. The road to the important city of Milan was now open. And Napoleon felt that something had changed in his view of himself: He would later recall that "it was only on the evening of Lodi that I believed myself a superior man, and that the ambition came to me of executing the great things which so far had been occupying my thoughts only as a fantastic dream."[20]

Conquest and Challenge

Conquering a land is one thing; managing its people so they are a help rather than a

Citizens of Milan welcome the triumphant Napoleon into their city, grateful for being liberated from Austrian rule.

hindrance to one's plans is another. Napoleon may have become disillusioned with the methods the French revolutionaries used to put their idealism into practice. He was quite willing, however, to use the ideas of liberty and reform to try to portray himself as a liberator of the oppressed. The following rather grandiose proclamation is a good example:

People of Italy! The French Army has just broken your chains of bondage. The French people are the friends of all peoples. Have confidence and work with us. Your property, your religion, and your customs will be respected.[21]

The reality was rather different. When Napoleon's army entered the rich city of Milan, the people cheered him for freeing them from Austrian rule. But,

instead of taking advantage of the goodwill of this large, prosperous capital, Napoleon, at the urging of the French commissars, including Salicetti, unleashed thousands of hungry, tired, victorious, womanless troops on the unsuspecting people of Milan, who became victims of an orgy of destroying, rapine, and killing. He had promised his men riches . . . and now they were taking him at his word.

After veritable fortunes were stolen from the private citizens of this city in "war contributions," another ten million

Conditions in Military Hospitals

In Napoleon Bonaparte, *Alan Schom quotes a letter written to Napoleon by Jean-Baptiste Turiot, a young surgeon serving with the army in Italy.*

This month, even as the preliminary treaties [ending the war] are being signed at Leoben, our hospitals are still filled . . . with 25,000 ill and wounded men. . . . And yet most of the sick are the result of poor hygiene, contaminated or insufficient food, unhealthful camps, and the miasma [disease-laden fog] of surrounding swamps. . . . [The present situation would not exist] if the wounded were not herded into wretched hovels and then forced to lie on damp stone or earth floors without mattresses, without covers, without even the most elementary care and attention that common decency requires. [Because of the lack of food in our hospitals] the men are literally dying of hunger before our eyes. At Bazzola a poor hospital porter gave three francs of his own money to buy a little food in order to save the lives of men dying of starvation.

Like an enormous fire, typhus is sweeping our hospitals and barracks. . . . Typhus, the mortal plague afflicting all campaigning armies, is caused by the filth of these quarters, the lack of fresh air, the negligence of the troops [in their personal hygiene], and the total lack of concern by our own general staffs. Indeed, even in our hospitals in Milan, . . . the wounded and sick are relegated to disgusting places and denied any sort of help because the war commissars . . . have stolen and sold army medical supplies, down to the very hospital mattresses."

livres were taken from the dukes of Parma and Modena. And then the trains of war booty—gold, silver, jewels, and works of art—soon to be synonymous with the name of Bonaparte were making their long journey over the Alps to Paris.[22]

When the Italians revolted against the French occupation, they were brutally suppressed. Back home, French officials eagerly refilled the nation's empty treasury—and Napoleon and his generals did not neglect to fill their own pockets as well.

Napoleon pushed on toward Mantua, the headquarters of the Austrian forces in northern Italy. The city was guarded by twelve thousand soldiers and surrounded by disease-ridden swamps. While besieging Mantua, Napoleon sent forces into central Italy to the states ruled by the pope, demanding money, supplies, and cannon—which were hauled up to Mantua to help with the siege.

Napoleon's happiness with his success was marred only by the unresponsiveness of his wife. Everyday he wrote lovesick letters to Joséphine; however she was much more interested in the social life of Paris (and, unknown to Napoleon, she was carrying on an affair with a young army lieutenant). Despite his pleas, Joséphine delayed going to Milan to join her husband.

Meanwhile, the Austrians sent a large army to Mantua in an attempt to lift the siege. General Dagobert Siegmund von Wurmser's main army headed for the city while a smaller force tried to cut Napoleon's supply lines. Napoleon used the same tactics he had employed successfully earlier: He blocked Wurmser, pushed the two armies apart, and destroyed the smaller force at Lonato in early August.

Then, at Castiglione della Stiviere, some fifteen miles north of Mantua, he defeated Wurmser and forced him to retreat. The Austrian force broke through into Mantua but was trapped there.

Hard fighting continued as 1796 drew to a close. Yet another large Austrian army, this one commanded by Baron Nicholas von Alvinzi, came into play. At first it met with success, pushing aside General Masséna and bruising Napoleon's army, which had shrunk to only thirteen thousand tired men. Napoleon rallied his troops, however, telling them that one more good push would turn things around.

Preparing to swing around Arcola to strike the rear of the much larger Austrian army, his attack ground to a halt at a key river crossing. As Austrian fire swept the bridge, Napoleon tried to lead the attack as he had at Lodi, but he slipped and fell into the swamp and had to be pulled out by two of his officers. Finally, on the fourth day of the battle, Napoleon and Masséna were able to push their way across. With both sides near exhaustion, the French beat the Austrians at Rivoli Veronese in January 1797. Then, turning back on Mantua, they obtained the surrender of the bulk of the Austrian forces.

New Tactics

Despite the false starts and setbacks, Napoleon was developing the sense of timing that would enable him to land the final, decisive blow. Or, to use a different sports metaphor, one writer has noted that "the American baseball analyst Bill James may have come close to one secret when he wrote, half jokingly, that Napoleon in-

Napoleon carries the French flag into battle at Arcola, Italy. Napoleon's superior warfare tactics won the battle, securing French dominance in Italy.

vented relief pitching: the strategy of saving the best troops for the late innings."[23]

In addition, the rules of the game seemed to be changing. As writer Albert Sidney Britt notes in his book *The Wars of Napoleon,*

> the Battle of Arcola was a radical departure from the type of battle that had been fought before the Revolution by generals like Marlborough [in 1704] and Frederick the Great [during the Seven Years War of 1756–1763]. For one thing, Arcola lasted three days, while Blenheim, Prague, and Leuthen were one-day fights. Second,

tactics at Arcola were largely a matter for division commanders, while in the old style of warfare, in which an army fought in one solid mass, the army commander specified formations, routes of advance, time of attack, etc. for every battalion of the army. At Arcola, even small unit commanders and individual soldiers had to exercise initiative. . . . Also, individual soldiers had to fight on their own in the swampy, dike country between the Alpone and Adige Rivers. Parade formations had no place on this kind of terrain, where the best techniques were patrols, sniping, bushwhackings, and aggressive small-unit skirmishes.[24]

When the French showed that they were prepared to invade Austria, the two nations signed the Treaty of Campo Formio. Thus, as of October 18, 1797, France became the dominant power in Italy.

In 1799 Austrian and Russian troops temporarily regained control of Italy; but the following year, Napoleon and General Louis-Alexandre Berthier made the difficult journey through the Great St. Bernard pass and fought a desperate campaign to retake the territory. On June 14, 1800, near the town of Marengo, the force under General Berthier was surprised by General Michael Melas's thirty-one thousand Austrian troops backed by one hundred cannon. At first Napoleon mistakenly thought this was only a diversionary attack, and he detached some of Berthier's troops. Then the truth dawned that this was the main battle, and he was badly outnumbered. By three o'clock that afternoon, Napoleon was almost ready to concede defeat.

But General Desaix de Veygoux arrived in the nick of time, making the famous

Time Is of the Essence

Since Napoleon was one of history's most successful generals, many of Napoleon's maxims, or pithy sayings, have become part of military lore. Many of them, like those collected by Philip J. Haythornthwaite and his coeditors in Napoleon: The Final Verdict *had to do with the importance of speed and time.*

"The strength of an army, like the power in mechanics, is estimated by multiplying the mass by the rapidity; a rapid march augments the morale of an army; and increases all the chances of victory."

"Strategy is the art of making use of time and space. I am less [worried about] the latter than . . . the former; space we can recover, time never."

"Time is the great element between weight and force."

"It may be that in the future I may lose a battle, but I shall never lose a minute."

Well known for both his battles and his maxims, Napoleon remains a larger-than-life figure in history.

comment that "this battle is lost, but there is still time to win another."[25] With Desaix de Veygoux's fresh troops smashing into the Austrians and Kellermann's experienced cavalry hitting them in the flank, the French turned the tide and forced the Austrians to give up northern Italy.

Most Italians had mixed feelings about the war. Many citizens desired national independence, which would not be granted under Napoleon. He did, however, establish two satellite republics (the Ligurian and Cisalpine in Lombardy) that represented the first French attempts to bring reform to conquered territory. In these republics, Italians were exposed to the relatively liberal French law and institutions. Between 1800 and 1814, the French annexed Piedmont, Genoa, and some smaller states (including the papal states) directly to France. In addition, Napoleon carved out the Kingdom of Italy, which he ruled as king, and the Kingdom of Naples, which would first be ruled by Napoleon's brother Joseph.

These larger states gave Italian nationalists the hope of eventual unity, but in 1814, after the downfall of Napoleon, the Congress of Vienna tried to restore the old states and the dominance of Austria. The spirit of nationalism and reform did not die, however. A series of revolts would eventually create new republics by mid-century and a united Kingdom of Italy in 1861.

The Triumphant Warlord

The Napoleon who returned to Paris in December 1797 was a far cry from the artillery commander who had dutifully saved the government two years earlier. In his headquarters in Italy he had appeared to visitors to be more like a prince with a splendid court than a mere field commander. Napoleon clearly liked the power and scope for action that his victories had brought him. "I have tasted command," he said in his diaries. "I cannot give it up."[26] And he had told his intimate friends about much more ambitious plans:

"What I have done so far is nothing," he said to us; "I am but at the opening of the career I am to run. Do you suppose that I have gained my victories in Italy in order to advance the lawyers of the Directory . . . ? Do you think, either, that my object is to establish a Republic? What a notion! A republic of thirty million people, with our morals and vices! How could that ever be? It is a chimera [unrealized dream] with which the French are infatuated but will pass away in time like all the others. What they want is glory and the gratification of their vanity; as for liberty, of that they have no conception."[27]

While the triumphant general was being wined and dined in Paris, the Directory had good reason to be nervous. As historian Michael Rapport notes, the political situation had become quite unstable:

With war raging in Europe and unrest at home, the Directory faced determined opposition from the radical Jacobins on the Left and Royalists on the Right. In western France, the Catholic Royalist rebellion, the Chouannerie, remained a festering wound. Elsewhere in France the dodging of conscription, desertion from the army and brigandage [highway robbery by organized gangs] ensured that the regime had a hard task in restoring order to the countryside. Its failure to do so did little to reassure property owners, who of course included some of the peasantry. Much of the peasantry also resented the continuing persecution of the Catholic clergy, which stemmed from the Revolution's decision to reform the church and to nationalize its property in 1789. [Members of the clergy who opposed] settlement, became focal points for counter-revolution. Moreover, the Directory had inherited considerable financial problems.[28]

The Directory government had been bolstered by the wealth Napoleon had sent from Italy, but the general's very success posed the threat that he would use his army and his popular support to seize power.

Members of the Directory thought they had a safe way to manage Napoleon, however. With Austria defeated and Italy secure, the biggest long-term threat to France appeared to be Great Britain. The island nation's powerful navy controlled the seas, and the wealth it gained from industry and overseas trade gave the British government the money to support the armies of France's neighbors in their efforts to overrun the republic. So the Directory put Napoleon to the task of organizing an invasion of England.

Egyptian Interlude

Napoleon quickly realized that the proposed conquest would be hopeless, at least for the time being. Britain's navy could intercept and destroy any invasion fleet before it could cross the English Channel. Besides, the French were unprepared to handle the details of the invasion, lacking hundreds of boats necessary to haul the soldiers, cannon, and supplies to Great Britain. Instead, Napoleon, supported by Foreign Minister Charles-Maurice de Talleyrand-Perigord, proposed an invasion of Egypt.

Why Egypt? If successful, the invasion would force the British to divert many of their ships and troops to protect their interests in the Middle East. This in turn might leave the British coast vulnerable to invasion. Also, a French army in Egypt could then eventually strike toward India,

threatening Britain's rich trade there. Privately, the Directory no doubt thought of a third advantage: Napoleon would be far from Paris and it could postpone sharing power with him. Napoleon was quite aware of this, of course:

They don't want any part of me. . . . They must be overthrown . . . but the time is not yet ripe. . . . I've taken certain soundings. . . . I would be standing all alone. Very well, then, we will go to Egypt after all, that is where all the great opportunities for glory lie. . . . I am going to dazzle that lot yet! [29]

Napoleon's enthusiastic sales pitch to the Directory had pointed out that the Mamluks, the warrior class who ruled feudal Egypt, would be no match for a modern army and the oppressed Egyptian people would rise up and support the French. As a bonus, the "insulting" behavior that the Ottoman Empire had shown toward France in the past could be punished. Napoleon made it sound quite easy.

According to Alan Schom, however,

the fact of the matter is that not just the landing but the entire campaign was a colossal foul-up from the very beginning, in consequence of Bonaparte's haste and oversights. It was a move at once as arrogant as it was irresponsible, and every member of his expedition was to suffer accordingly. In reality Napoleon knew little more than where the main cities of Egypt were located. For the most part, he did not know the location of the main food storage depots, wells, and cisterns along his proposed invasion route—and this during the hottest month of the year. And yet on the actual march inland, Napoleon brought almost no supplies of food or water, intending instead for the troops to "live off the land." Such a plan would have been difficult even in Europe. This, however, was not bountiful Europe, but a vast desert.[30]

This would not be the first time Napoleon, a master of tactics, would misjudge the strategic factors of climate, geography, and culture that could determine the long-term success or failure of a campaign.

Alexandria

In May 1798 Admiral Brueys's armada of 85 warships and 130 transports carrying Napoleon's 38,000 troops and thousands of support personnel sailed out of Toulon into the Mediterranean. Meanwhile, the British navy, suspecting that a major French effort was underway, ordered Admiral Horatio Nelson to locate and destroy the French fleet.

Searching the seas around Italy, Nelson came to suspect that the French might be heading for Egypt. In fact, on June 23 the two fleets missed each other by seventy-eight miles (as determined by historians from the navigational coordinates recorded in the two admirals' logs). Nelson ordered full sail for Alexandria, Egypt, and arrived there a day *ahead* of the French fleet. Seeing the fleet was not there, he doubled back and narrowly missed it once more. (When Nelson later learned of these missed opportunities, he exclaimed: "The devil's children have the devil's luck!"[31])

Anxiously scanning the horizon for British ships that might appear at any mo-

English admiral Horatio Nelson (pictured) was ordered to destroy the French fleet and prevent Napoleon from gaining more territory.

ment, the French soldiers climbed down into boats and prepared to land near Alexandria. Unfortunately, a sudden storm brought high winds and choppy seas. The combination of bad weather and the troops' inexperience with amphibious operations resulted in chaos, with dozens dead and injured. Even when the bulk of the force had landed, the French found they could not lower their cannon or horses into the boats, so the attack on Alexandria would have to proceed without artillery or cavalry.

Despite their rocky start, the French columns successfully fought off attacking Bedouin (nomadic Arab) cavalry, exchanged fire with the defenders on the city walls, and broke into and captured the famous, ancient city of Alexandria on July 2.

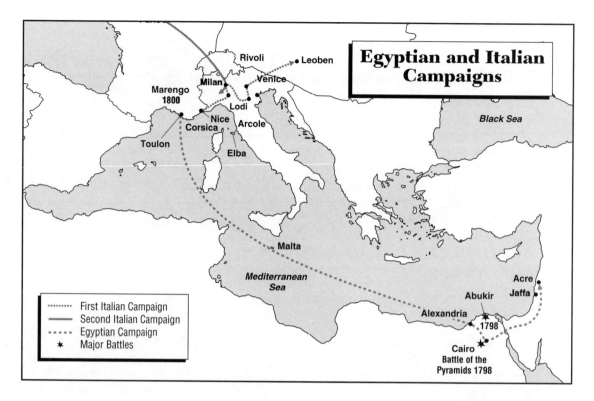

Egyptian and Italian Campaigns

Rivoli
Leoben
Marengo 1800
Milan
Venice
Lodi
Nice
Corsica
Arcole
Toulon
Elba
Black Sea
Malta
Mediterranean Sea
Acre
Abukir
Jaffa
Alexandria
1798
Cairo
Battle of the Pyramids 1798

········· First Italian Campaign
———— Second Italian Campaign
- - - - Egyptian Campaign
 ★ Major Battles

The Napoleonic propaganda machine immediately went into high gear to take advantage of the Egyptian people's dislike of the Mamluks who had ruled them harshly for generations. Napoleon informed the inhabitants that "I have come to restore your rights and to punish the usurpers. I respect God, his prophet, Muhammad, and the Koran far more than the Mamelukes do."[32] Napoleon tried to suppress looting, though not always successfully. His assurances convinced the Egyptian leaders to support the French conquest of the rest of Egypt.

The French position in Alexandria was isolated and precarious, however. Located on a long spit of land, the city can easily be cut off by a naval raid. Napoleon quickly pushed inland to make his position more secure. Unfortunately, as historian C. de la-Jonquière later described,

within three hours of leaving Alexandria [for Rosetta, about fifty miles to the east], any semblance of marching order had disappeared. Scarcely one and a half miles from Alexandria one entered the desert, and by 10 A.M. the heat became so oppressive, and our thirst so great there amid the sand dunes, without water, that men were collapsing every step of the way . . . and later we were told that three had already died of thirst.[33]

And that was only the first few miles of what would turn out to be a trek of hundreds of miles.

Despite the harsh conditions, the French forces continued southward. Fierce bands of Mamluk cavalry charged the French columns. The well-drilled soldiers, however, quickly formed a square formation, presenting a wall of musket fire and bayonets to the oncoming horsemen. The square held, and the French defeated the Egyptians in the Battle of the Pyramids and captured the city of Cairo on July 21.

The following week, however, Nelson's British fleet arrived at Abukir Bay, where the French had moored their ships. Since there were not enough sailors left on the ships to sail them, Admiral Brueys ordered the men to fight from anchor, thus giving the British the crucial advantage of mobility. Nelson boldly ordered his ships to come at the French line at a right angle, with a pair of British ships engaging each French warship. This allowed them to rake the French with gunfire from both sides while far fewer French guns could bear on the British. Despite the bravery of the French crews, the British captured most of the French battleships in this encounter, which is known to history as the Battle of the Nile. In his reports to Paris, Napoleon blamed Admiral Brueys for not having moved his ships from Abukir Bay to the more protected harbor of Alexandria. This was unfair, however: Alexandria's harbor was not deep enough to safely accommodate the warships.

A Shattered Dream

The rest of the campaign was a disaster. When the Ottoman Empire declared war on the French, Napoleon attacked them in Palestine, capturing Jaffa but ending up besieged in Acre as the British reinforced their Turkish allies. A thrust into Syria also failed. When the British landed fifteen thousand Turks near Alexandria, Napoleon defeated them, but he realized that the isolated French could not hold out much longer.

For Napoleon, the whole campaign would be recalled as though it were a fantastic dream:

> The time which I passed in Egypt was the most delightful of my life. . . .

Napoleon during the Battle of the Pyramids in Alexandria, Egypt. The French boldly defeated the Mamluks and captured the important city of Cairo.

In Egypt I found myself free from the wearisome restraints of civilization. I dreamed all sorts of things, and I saw how all that I dreamed might be realized. I created a religion. I pictured myself on the road to Asia, mounted on an elephant, with a turban on my head, and in my hand a new Koran, which I should compose according to my own ideas. . . . I was to have attacked the English power in India, and renewed my relations with old Europe by my conquest. . . . Fate decided against my dream.[34]

Rather than picking up the pieces of his shattered dream, Napoleon found a couple of small, serviceable frigates and

French sailors pull their comrades out of the water as their flagship L'Orient *is destroyed during the Battle of the Nile.*

Nelson at Abukir Bay

In Napoleon Bonaparte, *Alan Schom describes the climax of the naval battle in which Horatio Nelson's English fleet stranded Napoleon's Egyptian expedition.*

"The high point of the fierce onslaught came at approximately 10:15 P.M., when [French admiral] Brueys' *Orient*, the pride of the navy, blew up with most of its crew and officers, causing a deafening explosion and the ground to tremble at [French] General Kléber's headquarters at Alexandria, more than fifteen miles away, where 'a bright flash of flame as big as a warship rising rapidly in the air' was seen against the night sky, 'the flame growing larger and larger, until it changed into a cloud of black smoke, mixed with showers of luminous sparks.' Lieutenant Maissin, a survivor of the tragedy, recalled: 'the explosion of the flagship was followed by a mournful silence, as both navies, struck with horror, ceased fire.'"

sailed for France, a lucky Mediterranean fog concealing him from the British patrols. When he hastily retreated from Egypt, he had left behind about a third of his army dead from wounds and disease; the surviving soldiers would eventually be returned to France after a peace treaty was signed with the British. The news of his defeat would take a long time to catch up with him, and by then it would no longer matter.

The encounter between Napoleon and Egypt would have important long-term consequences. Despite Napoleon's propaganda efforts, the people of the Nile had not really embraced the French. Nothing in the traditional Egyptian culture had prepared them to accept the French ideas of "liberty, equality, and fraternity." Moreover, as writer Mahmoud Hussein notes,

this army belonged to a country of which the collective Egyptian experience retained the most bitter memory, that of the pitiless confrontation between Christendom and Islam—the Crusades. With the exception of a minority of intellectuals, who were attracted by the secular French approach, the Egyptian people saw the French expedition as a new Crusade.[35]

Napoleon's attempts to impose modern French law came up against religious traditions, particularly with regard to marriage, the family, and property matters. However, after the French left and the Mamluks tried to reestablish their harsh rule, Egyptian thinkers and leaders began to use the French secular, liberal ideas to organize resistance. One such leader, Muhammad 'Ali Pasha, extensively modernized Egypt, reformed its legal and tax system, and brought the country well on the way to independence in the later nineteenth century.

3 Transforming the Republic: Napoleon Remakes France

To the Directory, Napoleon was a tool, but a very dangerous one. As one general noted privately: "The directors think that they are using him, but one fine morning he is going to gobble them up, without their being able to do anything about it."[36]

Support for the Directory government eroded steadily in 1799. The losses of French territory in Italy while Napoleon was in Egypt reflected badly on the leadership. But the Directory, having fattened its purse on Napoleon's plunder, had become committed to war as a permanent revenue source. As monarchist Mallet du Pan complained, "The French Republic is eating Europe leaf by leaf, like the head of an artichoke. It revolutionizes them that it may despoil them, and it despoils them that it may subsist."[37]

Meanwhile, the members of the Directory maintained a luxurious lifestyle in which bribery was "business as usual." To prevent financial collapse, the Directory made a deal with the more radical republicans who were waiting in the wings to seize power. With the support of the extremists, the Directory increased taxes and forced the bourgeoisie, who had supported it, to loan the government large sums of money. In exchange, the radicals were given free rein to revamp the education system and attack religion. Catholics

Surrounded by members of the Council of Five Hundred who have fled to St. Cloud, Napoleon is elected protector of the legislature.

and royalists responded by stirring up revolts in the provinces. In this atmosphere of chaos, several unsuccessful coups d'ètat were attempted.

In October 1799 Napoleon returned to Paris, where he was greeted by throngs of supporters who remembered his earlier amazing victories in Italy. He and Josèphine became reconciled, at least for a while. Napoleon then put out his political antenna and looked for an opportunity to gain political power. It was not long in coming.

One member of the Directory, Emmanuel-Joseph Sieyès, was ready to seize control of the state and establish a more conservative, efficient government. Napoleon told Sieyès he would be happy to help: "We have no government because we have no constitution, or at least not the one we need; your genius must give us one."[38] (One can almost hear Napoleon buttering up the older man, whose pamphlet "What Is the Third Estate?" had helped spark the revolution in 1789.)

In the first week of November a rumor spread that the radical leftists, or Jacobins, were preparing to organize a popular uprising against the government. Alarmed, the two legislative bodies (the Council of Ancients and the Council of Five Hundred) fled the city for the suburb of St. Cloud, and their leaders swore in Napoleon as their protector. Napoleon and General Pierre-François-Joseph Lefebvre went with five hundred troops to "protect" the legislators. Although some members protested the presence of the troops, the two bodies settled down to discuss and debate reform proposals as though nothing were happening.

Impatient, Napoleon went to address the Council of Ancients. "The Republic has no government; only the Council of Ancients remains," he shouted angrily. "I will be your agent in action. Let us save liberty! Let us save equality!"[39] But when he

---

The Levers of Power

In The Mind of Napoleon, *J. Christopher Herold describes Napoleon's attitude toward governance and offers supporting quotes from the emperor.*

"[For Napoleon] the art of government is to keep people reasonably happy by giving them what they want and to obtain from them all one can get. The good could be corrupted; as for the bad, 'a legislator must know how to take advantage of even the defects of those he wants to govern.'"

"Men are like ciphers [zeroes]: they acquire their value merely from their position."

"Men are moved by two levers only: fear and self-interest. To make them behave, one must play on both levers."

"The ruler must teach them respect ('Nothing is more salutary than a terrible example given at the right time.'), but the lesson must be given sparingly."

"The masses desire equality, but 'they would gladly renounce it if everyone could entertain the hope of rising to the top. . . . What must be done then is to give everybody the hope of being able to rise.'"

was asked about saving the constitution, Napoleon told the legislators that it was they who had repeatedly ignored it. A torrent of accusations and counter-accusations erupted, and Napoleon faltered and was led away by his aides.

First Among Equals

Napoleon knew he had to recover quickly from the rebuff. He went to the more radical legislature, the Council of Five Hundred, accompanied by four soldiers. He was greeted with cries of "Down with the dictator!" and again appeared to be disoriented. But his brother, Lucien Bonaparte, saved him by rallying the troops, who accompanied Napoleon once more into the chamber, bayonets extended. The opposition fled, some jumping through the windows, whereupon the Council of Ancients passed a resolution replacing the Directory with three "provisional consuls"—Napoleon, Sieyès, and Pierre-Roger Ducos, a member of the Council of Five Hundred.

Like much eighteenth-century political theory, this idea harkened back to the ancient Roman republic, which was jointly ruled by supposedly equal officials called consuls. Such arrangements are generally unstable, with one person becoming dominant. The new 1799 "Constitution of the Year VIII," written by Sieyès, gave the real power to the First Consul, who happened to be Napoleon. It also marked a departure from the revolutionary ideals of 1789: It did not speak of individual liberty or human rights, but rather guaranteed property and security. A decade of rebellions, coups, and repressions had created a deep longing for peace and security in the people. When the constitution was put to the vote, people accepted it by a reported margin of 3.5 million to fifteen hundred. (Taking no chances, Napoleon had made sure the election was rigged.)

Looking back, Napoleon insisted that what he had done was necessary to preserve France. "I closed the gulf of anarchy and cleared the chaos. I purified the Revolution."[40]

The original battle cry of the revolution had been "liberty, equality, fraternity." Napoleon believed that the people no longer cared about liberty: They wanted "equality" in the form of consistent laws, fair treatment, and the opportunity to be rewarded for excellence. "Fraternity" would become the bonding of citizens into a national identity. These two impulses would help fuel Napoleon's future efforts at conquest. Equality would help cultivate talented military officers and government officials who could efficiently administer the coming empire. Fraternity would motivate hundreds of thousands of new recruits for what would become the Grande Armée (Grand Army).

Reorganizing France

One of Napoleon's first reforms was to create a uniform system of political organization. Thus all France was divided into districts called *départements*, which in turn were divided into arrondissements, which were further divided into cantons and then into communes. (These divisions were roughly equivalent to counties, municipalities, and wards or parishes in the American system.)

Although the legislature had the power to vote (pictured), Napoleon held ultimate control over French politics.

All male adults could vote, but they voted directly only to choose one-tenth of the members of their commune, who in turn voted one-tenth of their number to the departmental list, who in turn voted one-tenth of their number to the national list (for nation-wide offices). The actual control was held by departmental prefects and arrondissement subprefects, both chosen by the interior minister. (The first person to hold this post was Napoleon's brother Lucien.) Even mayors of the cantons were chosen in Paris. As a result, the government was structured like a pyramid with power centralized at the top. And while the Revolution had abolished nobility, Napoleon re-created it in the form of the class of "notables"—persons distinguished by wealth or achievement.

But as the system worked out in practice, the people at the top of the voting pyramid had little power. The real power to make laws lay with Napoleon and his small group of advisers, the Council of State. The legislature continued to exist, to be sure. It was divided into three parts: the Senate, which could decide whether a given law was constitutional; the Tribunate, chosen by the Senate to discuss (but not to vote on) bills; and the Legislative Body, chosen by the Senate to vote on bills (but not to discuss them). This cumbersome political machinery seemed to be designed to hinder any who might try to organize opposition to Napoleon. At any rate, Napoleon used his power to pack the legislative bodies with his supporters.

The Napoleonic Code

Whether or not Napoleon considered democracy to be a good idea, he did care deeply about reforming the legal system so that it satisfied the people's need for security. He believed that a ruler could get away with measures that took away individual freedoms: "[The desire for liberty] can be repressed with impunity." He wrote, "Liberty means a good civil code. The only thing modern nations care about is property."[41]

After becoming First Consul, Napoleon implemented his Napoleonic Code, a legal system based on the equality of all citizens.

Protection of property kept factory owners, merchants, and investors happy. Happy businesspeople produced wealth, and wealth reduced social unrest and made the new large-sized armies possible.

The laws of the ancien régime, or feudal France, were a jumble of different codes. Laws in southern France traced their roots back to ancient Roman law, while in northern France the customary law of the Frankish and Germanic Middle Ages predominated.

The legal system of republican France, which became known as the Napoleonic Code, was based on the idea that all French citizens were equal before the law. Thus, by declaring that no citizen could claim for himself or herself a status higher than that of any other citizen, Napleon ef-

fectively abolished the traditional privileges of the hereditary nobility and the clergy. The code then systematically laid out the legal procedures involving marriage and family relations, property rights, and ways of transferring rights, such as by inheritance or through contracts.

Modern historians have been quick to point out that Napoleon's concept of equality was limited in important ways. In the French colony of Santo Domingo in the Caribbean, for example, Napoleon reimposed slavery to keep the support of wealthy plantation owners.

Closer to home, the new legal system took away many of the rights women had gained in the Revolution. As J. Christopher Herold points out, Napoleon had a view of women that would certainly be called "male chauvinism" today:

> Under the old regime married women had enjoyed wide freedom, separate property rights, and an influential place in society. The Revolution had widened their rights. Napoleon imposed on French society his view that women must be treated as irresponsible minors throughout their lives. "Women should stick to knitting," he once told the son of Madame de Staël [a famous intellectual who became one of Napoleon's most vocal critics], who is not known to have knitted much. To the Council of State he declared that "the husband must possess the absolute power and right to say to his wife: 'Madam, you shall not go out, you shall not go to the theatre, you shall not receive [entertain] such and such a person; for [in this way I can ensure that] the children you will bear shall be mine.'" [42]

The civil part of the Napoleonic Code also favored some people over others. In disputes between employers and workers, courts were to give employers the benefit of the doubt. Moreover, tradespeople and laborers were forbidden to form unions, and workers were required to carry passbooks issued by the local authorities—an innovation that would be adopted by more than one twentieth-century dictatorship.

Creating the Napoleonic Code was a monumental task that required endless meetings, many of which were attended by Napoleon himself and in which he showed surprising knowledge of legal nuances and considerable patience in prodding the lawyers to resolve disputes. The work demonstrated that Napoleon, at his best, was a superb administrator. According to one biographer,

Napoleon brought to the task of government exactly that assemblage of qualities which the situation required, an unsurpassed capacity for acquiring technical information in every branch of government, a wealth of administrative inventiveness which has never been equaled, a rare power of driving and draining the energies of man, a beautiful clearness of intellect which enabled him to seize the salient [outstandingly important] features of any subject, however tough, technical and remote, a soldierly impatience of verbiage in others combined with a serviceable gift of melodramatic eloquence in himself;

The "Black Napoleon"

In his memoirs, Napoleon writes about a plan that might have changed the destiny of the United States and the people of the Americas with the cooperation of Black leader Toussaint-Louverture. The latter was perhaps too much like Napoleon himself to be a suitable ally. This excerpt is from Somerset de Chair's Napoleon on Napoleon.

"[One alternative was to] invest General Toussaint-Louverture with the whole civil and military authority, under the title of governor-general of the colony; to entrust the command to the black generals. [If this were done] the Republic would have an army of from 25,000 to 30,000 blacks, which would make all America tremble: this would be a new element of power which would cost [France] no sacrifice, either of men or money. With [such an army], what might I not undertake against Jamaica, the Antilles, Canada, the United States themselves, or the Spanish colonies?

[But] Toussaint not only assumed authority over the colony during his life, but invested himself with the right of naming his successor; and pretended to hold his authority, not from the mother country but from a [so-called] colonial assembly which he had created."

above all, immense capacity for relevant labor."[43]

After it was proclaimed in 1804, the Napoleonic Code generally followed the armies into conquered territories and became the legal system for areas under French control, including parts of the Netherlands, Belgium, Italy, and Germany. (It even found its way to America, where the largely French-speaking inhabitants of Louisiana used the Napoleonic Code as the model for their 1825 Civil Code).

In reflections composed near the end of his life, Napoleon indicates that he thought very highly of his work for legal reform: "My real glory is not the forty battles I won—for my defeat at Waterloo will destroy the memory of those victories. . . . What nothing will destroy, what will live forever, is my Civil Code."[44]

Once he had gained control of the government as First Consul, Napoleon began to plan for the long-term stability of his regime. He was perhaps the first modern leader to consciously plan a state education system designed to develop young people into loyal citizens. His reforms included a standardized curriculum for all grades supervised by experts at the newly established University of Paris. Textbooks were also reviewed by the state and teachers licensed. (Later in the nineteenth century, Prussia and other European states would develop similar systems.)

Napoleon also dealt with the troublesome question of the relationship between church and state. The Revolution had led to the seizure of most church property, the closing of church schools, and the end to state-paid salaries for clergy. Resentment of these measures had fueled many of the royalist revolts against the republic. Unlike the radicals, however, Napoleon had no strong feelings against religion. As he would note in his memoirs:

> my policy is to govern men the way the majority wishes. That, I believe, is how one recognizes a people's sovereignty. By becoming Catholic I won the war in the Vendée, by becoming Moslem I established myself in Egypt, and by becoming an ultramontane [supporter of

Napoleon (back row, second from left) looks on as his civil code is presented to the Council of State. In addition to the Napoleonic Code, the new consul also created a national education system and reformed the church.

In The Age of Napoleon *the Durants record a woman turning the tables on Napoleon in conversation.*

"When [Napoleon] told a famous beauty, 'Madame, I do not like it when women mix in politics,' she retorted, 'You are right, General; but in a country when they have their heads cut off, it is natural that they should want to know why.'"

the Pope] I won people's hearts in Italy. If I were to rule over a Jewish nation, I would rebuild the temple of Solomon.[45]

Napoleon approached the pope in 1800 with a proposal to reconcile his regime with the church. This agreement, or concordat, was accepted on April 8, 1801, because it was valuable to both sides. The Catholic Church was granted freedom of worship and the right to appoint priests and have them paid by the state again. (None of the seized church property was to be returned, however.) In turn, Napoleon received an oath of loyalty from all bishops and priests and removed the clergy as a source of support for the royalists. Church services would include special prayers for the success of the regime, and the catechism now included the following question:

Question: What should one think of those who fail in their duties to our emperor?

Answer: According to the Apostle Saint Paul, they would resist the order established by God Himself and would make themselves deserving of eternal damnation.[46]

Although Napoleon and the pope would soon clash again, Napoleon would continue to receive most of the benefits of the new arrangement.

The First Modern Police State

While Napoleon made a considerable effort to inspire loyalty, he relied, as well, on coercion and heavy-handed measures. By the end of 1800 he had shut down sixty-four of the nation's seventy-three newspapers, the majority owned by royalists. The government had the *Moniteur* as its semi-official newspaper. All newspapers had to submit articles to the government censors before printing.

The powerful police minister Joseph Fouché placed agents and informants everywhere, rooting out suspected royalists and other enemies of the state. Since the judges were appointed and paid by Napoleon, the outcome of any trial for subversion was seldom in question.

As Fouché confidently reported to Napoleon,

Napoleon meets with the pope in an attempt to reconcile his government with the church. Their resulting concordat gave the church freedom of worship and Napoleon the church's loyalty.

we have all [the dissidents'] movements, words, acts, and most secret plans under the closest scrutiny, preparatory to penetrating their groups and arresting them. Every means of surveillance is available to the police, whose love for our nation renders this surveillance and its enforcement more sweeping, faster, and more infallible.[47]

Only the lack of modern telephone and radio communications limited the scope of the police and government agents.

Emperor Napoleon I

In August 1802 Napoleon had the rubber-stamp Senate declare him to be "First Consul for Life," with the right to name his successor. In effect, he was now king; but he was not a mere constitutional monarch because he also wrote a new "Constitution of the Year X" that gave him absolute power to make laws, interpret the constitu-

tion, and conduct wars and foreign policy. Napoleon had, apparently successfully, transformed the republican ideals of equality and fraternity while replacing liberty with dictatorship. The new monarchy was approved by the lopsided (and crooked) vote of 3,572,329 to 2,569.

Some opposition to the regime continued. Napoleon responded not by compromise but by promoting himself once again. The final step called for the elevation of the First Consul to the status of emperor. As one historian notes,

[Napoleon's] action [in making himself emperor] was influenced partly by the growth of opposition. Several attempts had recently been made to take his life, and royalist plots were being hatched against him. Napoleon proceeded against the conspirators with characteristic ruthlessness. Scores were arrested upon mere suspicion, and some of the most prominent were singled out for execution. Having thus disposed of his chief enemies, Napoleon evidently concluded that the best way to guard against future trouble would be to establish a dynasty of his own and thereby cut the ground from under all the Bourbon pretenders [relatives of Louis XVI who might have claimed the throne of France].[48]

Napoleon staged a splendid (and carefully orchestrated) coronation ceremony on December 2, 1804. Thousands of notables came from around France and from the courts of Europe, the carriages streaming toward the Cathedral of Notre Dame, which dominates the Ile de la Cité in the center of Paris.

Napoleon sat on a golden throne, holding in his hand a sword that had sup-

Looking regal in his laurel wreath and coronation robe, Napoleon claimed the French throne and the title Holy Roman emperor.

During his elaborate coronation as emperor, Napoleon crowns Joséphine the new empress while the pope and others look on.

posedly come down from Charlemagne, the father of France and the first Holy Roman emperor. On a smaller throne nearby was Joséphine, dazzling in makeup and jewels, to be made empress. Pope Pius VII was present, too, signifying the new concord between France and the Catholic Church. But when the time came, Napoleon placed the crown on his own head. There was to be no question that Napoleon himself, not the pope, was the source of his own kingship. He no doubt reflected on almost two thousand years of history as he went through the ceremony. After all, he wore the laurel crown as the new Caesar (his regiments would carry eagle standards like that of the Roman legions), and he would be the new Holy Roman emperor, the supreme secular authority in Christendom.

Chapter

4 Marching to Empire: Napoleon, Britain, and the German States

Seemingly secure on his throne and now the equal of any European king, Napoleon announced to foreign diplomats that there was no longer any need for war. He had told the Prussian ambassador that he wanted to turn now "to the benefit of agriculture, industry, commerce, and the arts all those [financial] resources which war at once absorbs and besmirches." [49]

France and its neighbors had been at peace since the signing of the Treaty of Amiens with England on March 27, 1802. But the peace had lasted only a bit more than a year. Britain was reluctant to return any of the overseas colonies it had seized during the war, particularly Malta. Similarly, Napoleon did not withdraw occupation troops as agreed, and he signed a

Napoleon parades through the streets of Paris on review for his subjects. The new emperor quickly began establishing an empire after his coronation.

defense pact with a Swiss government he had largely created. Napoleon also worked to dismantle the remains of the old Holy Roman Empire so it would come under French rather than Austrian control. Napoleon's ambitions seemed clear. After all, it was unlikely that the kind of person who would crown himself an emperor would not want an empire.

Britain vs. France

If there had been no provocations, however, both Napoleon and the British leaders would have had to invent some. At first glance, France's nearly 30 million population in 1800 gave it a considerable advantage over England's 10 million; but Britain and France were on an economic collision course. While the island nation had only a small army, its worldwide trading network, protected by its navy, brought it great wealth. Further, Britain far outstripped its continental rival in implementing the Industrial Revolution in manufacturing. (On average, Britain annually produced 16 million tons of coal to France's 1 million, and it led in iron production 248,000 tons to 200,000, and in cotton consumption 32,000 tons to 8,000.) Further, about 17 percent of the British people lived in towns of 20,000 people or more, while only about 7 percent of the French population was urbanized. And London, the largest city in Europe at a population of 1.1 million, was nearly double the size of Paris.

Looking back after the war, the English economist Thomas Malthus noted that "In carrying the late war, we were powerfully assisted by our steam engines."[50] He also noted that "there [has never] been so rapid an increase of production and consumption as in the twenty-two years ending with 1814."[51] French experts were aware that they had to strike at Britain before its advantage increased. As Honoré Gabriel, marquis de Mirabeau, declared, "The enmity of England will be eternal; it will grow each year with the productivity of its industry, and even more than our own."[52]

By May 1803 war between France and Britain was again under way. It was mainly an economic war at first, though there were cannons at the business end. The British seized French ships in British-controlled ports and on the high seas. The French in turn arrested British citizens in French territory. French troops occupied Hannover (a German principality belonging to the English king). They ordered the Dutch to turn over their ships to France and began to coordinate with Spain, which was a French ally at the time and had been raided by British ships.

All this time Napoleon had been preparing a huge invasion force to sail from northern France across the channel to England, the move first proposed by the Directory some half-dozen years ago. An army of 150,000 had been assembled and hundreds of flatboats and gunboats had been built. (It is fortunate these vessels were never used because they lacked keels to stabilize them and would probably have sunk in the rough water of the English Channel.)

Napoleon believed that once his plans took full shape,

the English will find themselves simultaneously attacked in Asia, Africa, and America. These successive shocks at the main points of their [global] commerce will make them realize at long last just how very vulnerable they really

Keeping Healthy Till "Boney" Comes

The following instructions, excerpted from Philip J. Haythornthwaite's The Napoleonic Sourcebook, *were given to British volunteers who were being assembled to fight off Napoleon's expected invasion.*

"Wear Jersey shirts or flannel waistcoats and drawers, next to the skin; but in Spring and Summer, cotton and calico. In the night, always wear a double cotton or worsted nightcap, either in camp or cantonments [field encampments].

Bread, meat, and potatoes give and preserve robust muscular strength. Greens and fruits should be sparingly used, lest they produce fluxes [diarrhea]. Good malt liquor well hopped is excellent, but in cold weather, an addition of a little brandy, rum, or gin will be expedient [useful].

Smoking tobacco in cold weather, and in the night is useful and an excellent preservative. In case of putrid infection, disease, or fever, free air and vitriolic acid, bark and snakeroot are most certain remedies."

are. After these sweeping operations in the Caribbean and Africa, they will certainly not be expecting anything else. It will be easy to surprise them. . . . The Grande Armée de Boulogne. . . will then enter the county of Kent [on the southern coast of England].[53]

Napoleon devised a plan to distract the British navy by sending the French fleet under Admiral Villeneuve to the Caribbean, where he hoped the British fleet would follow. If so, the British coast would be left unguarded and open to the invasion fleet. The plan required incredible coordination: The British ships would have to be decoyed, and at the same time hundreds of flat-bottomed boats, some laden with artillery, would have to be launched on the same tide under cover of darkness to cross the English Channel.

Meanwhile, panic and national pride mingled as the British prepared to meet the expected invasion. In the pubs, people sang patriotic songs:

Bright honor now calls each true Briton to arm
Invasion's the word which hath spread the alarm
Bonaparte, and his legions, threaten us hard,
Yet their threats and bravados we [never] need regard
[Chorus]
Then stand up, bold Britons, for children and wives
In defence of Old England to venture your lives
Subscriptions now rise thro' the country at large,
To King and to Country their duty discharge;

For freedom we fight, and our cause it is just,
On our army and navy, we place our whole trust.[54]

Some witty person even made up a "wanted" poster describing the following criminal suspect:

A certain ill-disposed Vagrant and common Disturber, commonly called or known by the name of NAPOLEON BONAPARTE, alias Jaffa Bonaparte, alias Opium Bonaparte . . . [who] hath been guilty of divers [various] Outrages, Rapes, and Murders. [It is ordered that he] be forthwith sent to our Jail for WILD BEASTS . . . with the Ouran Outang, or some other ferocious and voracious animals like himself.[55]

As the small professional army was joined by volunteers drilling on village greens, and gun batteries were set up along the coast, the navy stepped up its level of alertness.

In March 1805 the French fleet made its decoy run out into the Atlantic, and British admiral Horatio Nelson took the bait. Unfortunately the invasion flotilla was nowhere near ready, and Napoleon became uncharacteristically hesitant. Admiral Villeneuve's French fleet was ordered to return. The admiral, afraid to confront Nelson closer to England, sailed for the coast of Spain in August.

Napoleon knew little about ships and naval operations. He felt that admirals such as Villeneuve were always making excuses about winds and tides and such, always coming up with a reason why the fleet could not sail when he wanted it to. (Since Napoleon's army had overcome snowy mountain passes in Italy and burning sands in Egypt, he assumed that the navy, too, could fight off contrary winds if they only had sufficient will.)

Napoleon now ordered Villeneuve to sail to the Spanish harbors of Cádiz and El Ferrol, collect the Spanish and French ships wintering there, and then sail along the French Atlantic coast to Brest and Boulogne, and then into the English Channel. "If you make me master [of the English Channel] for just three days," Napoleon declared, "with God's help I shall put an end to the destiny and existence of England."[56]

The Battle of Trafalgar

But Villeneuve's half-hearted performance in skirmishes with the British, combined with his failure to follow orders, led Napoleon to scrap the invasion plans and order the admiral's replacement. But before this could be done, Villeneuve sailed the fleet out of Cádiz harbor on his own initiative. Off Cape Trafalgar, which lies slightly northwest of the Strait of Gibraltar, Admiral Nelson's fleet of twenty-seven battleships attacked Villeneuve's thirty-two battleships. J. Christopher Herold describes the action:

Admiral Villeneuve accepted the battle with the full conviction that he was doomed. Aboard the British ships, morale was high to the point of exaltation. At 11 A.M. on October 21—a gray and squally morning—the *Victory* [flagship] signaled Nelson's message to his ships: "England expects that every man will do his duty." With their bands playing and the crews cheering, the ships bore down on the French. Nelson's plan was to cut the French line in three, then concentrate on the French rear and center. The *Royal Sovereign*, Admiral Collingwood's flagship, was the first to penetrate the French line; the *Victory*, with equal impetuousness, broke through behind the tenth French ship shortly afterward.[57]

The French and Spanish crews fought bravely, but when the fierce battle ended, the British had not lost a single ship, while twenty-two French and Spanish ships had been captured and the rest were fleeing for safety. (Nelson, however, did not survive the battle. The admiral's habit of wearing his gaudy uniform on the flagship's deck made him an excellent target for French snipers, and he died a few hours after being hit by a musket ball.)

Echoes in America

While the Napoleonic Wars were centered on Europe and its surrounding seas, the economy of the late eighteenth and early nineteenth centuries was already global in scope. Great Britain had largely superseded Spain and Portugal as the world's premier colonial power. Its trading network, which largely incorporated most of the Americas, was vital to the economies of many nations.

The independence of the United States represented the first departure from colonialism in the New World. Many American intellectuals and political leaders were sympathetic to the French Revolution and the new French republic during its early years. After all, the French revolutionaries had used stirring language that echoed the American Declaration of Independence. Thus people in the United States hoped that the French, too, would be able to establish a secure republic. Americans were also very grateful for the financial and military help that the French had provided during the Revolutionary War. Without it, most agreed, America would still be a British colony.

However, the increasing violence of the French Revolution, its radical language,

The superior English fleet devastates its opponents, leaving French and Spanish crews to perish in the waters off Cape Trafalgar.

A wounded Horatio Nelson collapses in the arms of his crew during the Battle of Trafalgar. The daring English admiral would not survive the battle.

ships. Skirmishes between American and French sailors in the Atlantic increased. The possibility of a pro-French revolutionary movement on American soil led to the passage of the Alien and Sedition Acts. Thomas Jefferson, who was much more sympathetic to the French, saw this legislation as a betrayal of American liberty and freedom of speech. In 1800, however, both sides in the undeclared war had had enough and signed a peace treaty.

In 1803 Napoleon realized that war with Britain was imminent. Whatever success France had gained in establishing its colonial presence in Santo Domingo and elsewhere in the Americas was likely to end once the British fleet intervened. Therefore, he sold the Louisiana Territory he had acquired from Spain to the United States. This transaction, agreed to on May 3, 1803, netted Napoleon about $15 million in funds for his war chest. The United States received a huge territory stretching

The violence of the French Revolution roused anti-French sentiment in the states, causing U.S. president George Washington and other Americans to avoid involvement in the affair.

and especially the execution of the king and queen turned many Americans against the French republic. America's first president, George Washington, was much more comfortable dealing with the British, and his attempts to avoid "entangling alliances" between America and European powers were interpreted by the French as ingratitude. In Paris the crude shaking down of American ambassadors for bribes by Napoleon's minister Talleyrand-Perigord did not help matters, either. John Adams used these events to stir up anti-French sentiment and to help the Federalist Party gain the White House in 1797.

As the French began to raid American ships, the United States also began to build a small navy and to arm its merchant from the Mississippi River to the foothills of the Rockies.

Most Americans would have been content to explore and settle this vast new land, but the importance of overseas trade dragged them back into the Napoleonic Wars. With Napoleon's Berlin Decree in 1806 and the British Orders in Council in January 1807, each power essentially forbade American and other neutral ships to trade with the other power or any of its colonies, and both began to routinely seize American merchant ships. The result was a devastating blow to American commerce.

In response, Jefferson, who had succeeded Adams as president, persuaded Congress to pass the Embargo Act of 1807, which forbade any imports to America from Britain or France until the European powers allowed free passage for American shipping. He hoped this would force recognition of American trading rights, but Napoleon and the British continued to seize American ships bound for the other's ports, and the American businesses that depended on imports (mainly in New England) faced ruin. Finally, in May 1810 Congress passed a law that basically declared that if either Britain or France repealed their restriction on American ships, America would reward that country by agreeing not to trade with the other.

Napoleon then privately offered to repeal his trade restrictions if England did the same. If the British did not cooperate, Napoleon said, the Americans must boycott them. But having gained tentative American agreement, Napoleon failed to

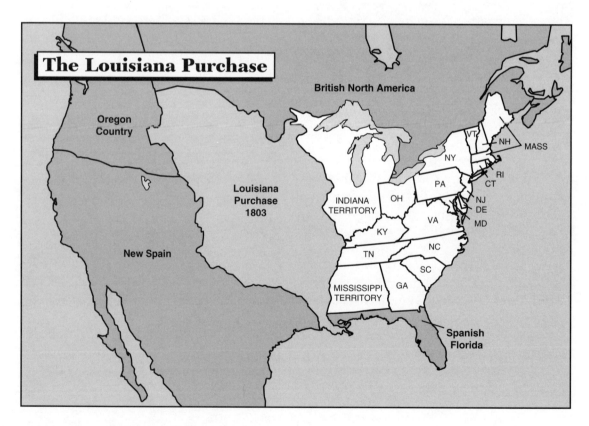

While France and Britain were waging war, American merchant ships were caught in the crossfire. In response, U.S. president Thomas Jefferson urged Congress to pass the Embargo Act of 1807.

follow through by issuing a public decree, and the British refused to respond with nothing on the table. This made it look like Britain was the obstacle to securing American trading rights.

Largely as a result of Napoleon's trickery, the United States declared war against Britain in 1812. The war was unpopular in both America and England, and it was largely inconclusive: The Americans tried unsuccessfully to invade Canada several times but did win a naval battle on the Great Lakes. Fast, powerful American frigates fought successful duels with their smaller British counterparts.

When Napoleon was defeated in late 1813, however, Britain was free to deal with the American upstarts. King George III, whose forces the colonists had defeated in 1781, sent large numbers of ships and troops to America, raided coastal cities, and burned the White House and other buildings in Washington. But by the time it looked like Britain could win the war, it no longer had a reason to fight it, and a peace treaty was signed in early 1814. (Before news of the treaty arrived in America, an ill-advised attack by the British on New Orleans was repulsed in a bloody battle led by future president Andrew Jackson.)

The Americans emerged from their small part in the Napoleonic Wars with more territory and greater confidence in having held their own against the British. They also felt the beginnings of a desire to become masters of the Western Hemisphere.

The Spanish Colonies

Certainly European colonialism in the Americas was dying and leaving a power vacuum. The centuries-old Spanish empire in Mexico and Latin America was ruled from Spain by leaders interested only in how much treasure they could squeeze from the colonies. When Napoleon invaded Spain and seized control of the government, leaders such as Francisco de Miranda adopted republican ideas from France and began to organize revolts; British attempts to exploit this unrest were largely unsuccessful. But between 1809 and 1811, a series of revolutions swept through Spanish colonies in Central and South America. Although Spanish royalists suppressed some of these revolutions following the defeat of Napoleon, under inspired leaders such as Simon Bolívar the tide was clearly moving toward independence.

Dead and dying British soldiers are scattered across the battlefield at New Orleans during the War of 1812. America and Britain made peace in 1814.

In the Old World, colonization would last much longer, with the British holding onto India despite French attempts to ally with native leaders against the British.

Building the Grande Armée

After his plan to invade England fizzled, Napoleon took the large army he had assembled and reorganized and expanded it. The result was the Grande Armée. It consisted of seven army corps, each a self-contained grouping of infantry, artillery, and cavalry, that could operate independently or be combined into a huge force of 350,000 men.

As military expert John Prados points out,

creating "corps" of troops from different combat arms [infantry, cavalry, artillery] permitted Napoleon's forces to operate in a dispersed [spread out] fashion while retaining real striking power all along the front. The formation also enabled Napoleon to take his adversaries by surprise, such as in 1806, when he moved the Grand Army through the supposedly impassable Franconian Forest to defeat the Prussians at Jena. Innovations in logistics [movement of troops and supplies], by professionalizing French supply services and standardizing weapons and organizations, simplified Napoleon's arrangements to go on campaign. By having French armies live off the land as much as possible, Napoleon could cut himself loose from the traditional network of depots upon which armies had previously depended. The French also worked hard at accumulating basic information such as accurate maps of potential theaters [areas] of operations, a valuable form of intelligence that their opponents could seldom match.[58]

Much of the effectiveness of this vast yet flexible force came from the careful way Napoleon cultivated its leadership, creating the special office of marshal as a step beyond ordinary general. Historian Philip J. Haythornthwaite writes:

Napoleon understood that his assumption of the imperial mantle was not entirely approved of by key army leaders. Indeed, several of his atheist, republican generals could stomach his coronation's religious overtones only by fortifying themselves liberally with alcohol, cursing continuously [in stage whispers] during the proceedings, and making sardonic comments. But, by his swift stroke—today I am named Emperor, tomorrow I name you marshals—he co-opted potential opposition by offering the irresistible lure of a marshal's baton. So they may have cursed and complained, but they did so while proudly fingering their batons. Which of them—apprentice dyer Jean Lannes; Joachim Murat, an innkeeper's son originally destined for the church; would-be village baker Nicholas Soult—could have anticipated that he would rise so far.[59]

The marshals would get much of the glory, but this same idea of opportunity for people who showed merit extended down the ladder of ranks to people from more modest backgrounds. As Napoleonic scholar Geoffrey Ellis points out,

the officer corps of the Grand Army thus became a microcosm [miniature version] of Napoleon's plans for society at large: to blend the old nobility with the bourgeoisie [middle class] of talent into a new class of Imperial notables [distinguished persons].[60]

Finally, the army would rely on the draft, or conscription. As time passed and bloody, endless wars seemed to drag on, conscription would become less and less popular and more widely resisted.

The Third Coalition

Napoleon soon had an opportunity to put his new army to the test. All along he had been straining at the bounds set by earlier peace agreements, nibbling at Austrian territories in the Netherlands, northern Italy, and southern Germany. When he declared himself king of Italy and added Genoa to the French Empire, Austria declared war, and it was not alone. In 1805 Czar Alexander I of Russia formed an alliance with Britain and Austria known as the Third Coalition against France. The czar, whose ambitions rivaled Napoleon's, hoped to gain territories in Poland and Prussia as well as eventually breaking up the Turkish Ottoman Empire. Britain, willing to pay to keep Napoleon in check, offered the czar a generous subsidy of 1.25 million pounds for each 100,000 Russian troops in the coming war.

The Austrian plan called for a main force of ninety-four thousand under Archduke Charles to move into northern Italy to threaten Napoleon's holdings around

Milan. A second army of seventy-two thousand under the command of General Karl Mack would march into Bavaria along the south bank of the Danube River, where it might force Bavaria into alliance with Austria and then wait for the arrival of a large Russian army to reinforce it in October.

Mack, an energetic but unimaginative general, did not believe that Napoleon could move a large force into Bavaria before the Russians came. He pushed ahead toward Ulm. But while Napoleon offered an alliance to Prussia and gathered information from his scouts and spies, the Grande Armée was heading for a confrontation with the unsuspecting Mack. By September 24 Napoleon had figured out the Austrians' strategic plans. In a letter to Marshal Bernadotte, Napoleon wrote:

> The Emperor of Germany [i.e. Austria] has made no detachment onto the right bank of the Danube, and the Russians have not yet arrived. . . . If I have the good fortune to catch the Austrian army asleep on the Iler [River] and in the Black Forest for three or four more days, I shall have outflanked it, and I hope only the debris [riffraff] will escape.[61]

Napoleon's "Home Office"

In the article "Napoleon and His Men," found in Philip J. Haythornthwaite's Napoleon: The Final Verdict, *author James R. Arnold describes Napoleon's meticulous travel arrangements.*

"In order to utilize efficiently his travelling time, Napoleon had a large coach which served as a mobile office. Its seat was divided by a low partition to allow him and a passenger, generally [Marshal] Berthier, to work without inconvenience. Facing the seat was a cabinet neatly compartmentalized with locking drawers to hold maps, files, and correspondence as well as open cupboards for food, drink, toiletries, paper, pens, telescopes, and a library. A sliding leaf pulled out from the cabinet provided a desk. A large, silver timepiece hung from a wall. At night a lantern illuminated the working surface from behind the passenger's shoulders. A rear trunk held bedding, extra torches, clothing. Beneath the coachman's seat was one of the Emperor's folding field beds which could be used to convert Napoleon's seat to a sleeping surface (poor Berthier had to sleep sitting up!). If a courier arrived, day or night, Napoleon could read his dispatches, consult any relevant files or maps, draft a response, have Berthier prepare the formal orders, and summon a fresh courier, all without stopping."

Following the advancing cavalry, Napoleon's troops crossed the Rhine. Meanwhile, Mack's force stumbled as it tried unsuccessfully to "live off the land" the way the French did. Mack suddenly realized he had been outflanked and retreated to Ulm, where he hoped to hold out until the Russians arrived. Napoleon did not realize at first that Mack was vulnerable, but when he discovered the opportunity, his corps closed the trap. Surrounded by two hundred thousand French troops, Mack's fifty thousand troops soon had to surrender. The approaching Russian general Mikhail Kutuzov, hearing of Mack's defeat, began to retreat, seeking a good defensive position where he could wait for another Russian army.

Austerlitz: Napoleon's Masterpiece

Napoleon then went on the offensive and headed for the Austrian capital of Vienna. He carefully set up defensive positions and supply routes to parallel the advance of his armies. Trusting Marshals Joachim Murat and Jean Lannes, he gave them the freedom to devise their own plans to catch Kutuzov's Russians. In one of miltary history's greatest con games, the marshals pretended that an armistice had been signed and conned the Austrians at the Tabor bridge, located to the east of Vienna, into letting the French forces across. The French then seized Vienna on November 12, but Napoleon was far from pleased when he arrived three days later because the marshals had let Kutuzov get away and join with the second Russian army.

Napoleon and his staff discuss their strategies at Austerlitz, where Napoleon would display his genius for warfare by setting an elaborate trap for the Russians and Austrians.

Napoleon, badly outnumbered, nevertheless gambled that the Prussians would not enter the war, and he called in two additional corps to face the combined Russian-Austrian force. As he set up his position, he led the enemy to assume that the French were confused by falling back from the town of Austerlitz. He even abandoned the commanding Pratzen Heights, allowing the Austrians to occupy it. He then deliberately weakened the

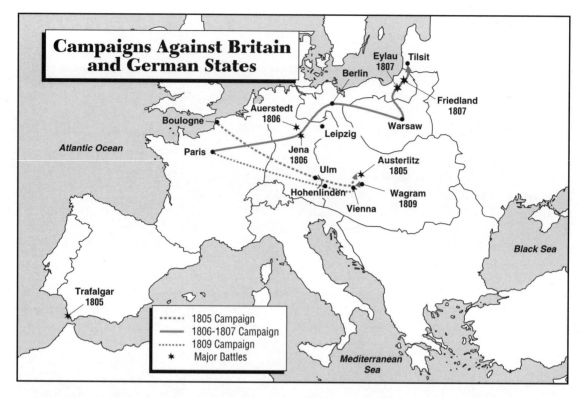

Campaigns Against Britain and German States

right flank of his line, while concealing a reserve force to the rear.

The allies took the bait, trying to flank the French and cut off their supply route from Vienna. Unknown to them, however, Napoleon had shifted his supplies to another road. When he learned of the allied movements, Napoleon exclaimed, "They are walking into the trap. Before tomorrow night this army will belong to me."[62]

As the allied attackers closed in, Napoleon rushed his concealed reinforcements into the line as well as charging the flank of the aggressors. Now the allies were sending more and more troops into the battle, stripping them from the high ground of the Pratzen Heights. Ever watchful, Napoleon picked his moment and sent his forces to retake the heights, cutting the connection between the allied left and center. Napoleon's forces could now defeat their enemies separately. Twenty-seven thousand allied soldiers were killed or wounded during the fighting; French losses totaled only about eight thousand. Austria was forced to sign an armistice and hand over Venice to France, and the Russians had to go home.

Now that Napoleon had beaten Austria decisively and sent the Russians packing, he was free to reorganize much of the Austrian kingdom. But Talleyrand-Perigord warned Napoleon that

> Your Majesty is now in a position to break the Austrian monarchy, or to support and re-erect it. Once broken, however, even Your Majesty will not possess power enough to reassemble the ruins of shattered states and to recompose it as the unit it formerly was.

And yet the existence of this single unit is most necessary. Indeed, it is quite indispensable for ensuring the future health of all civilized nations.

The Austrian monarchy . . . is a poorly composed mass of different states, almost all of them with their own languages, mores, religions, and political and civil system of administration, and whose only common link is their leader.

Today, defeated and humiliated, the Austrian Empire needs a generous, understanding hand from its conqueror.[63]

Napoleon seldom looked at long-term stability, however. Rather, he picked up shattered pieces of states and tried to link them into the patchwork fabric of his empire, often giving their thrones to members of his family. In this case, he carved pieces of Austria and gave them to his German allies, the electors of Württemberg and Bavaria. Historian Michael Broers observed that such policies became less successful as time passed:

> Napoleon sought to apply the same sets of policies to all the territories he came to control, regardless of when he seized them or whether he ruled them directly, as French departments, by proxy in his satellite kingdoms, or by indirect pressure, as in the independent, allied states of the Confederation of the Rhine. How successful he was depended essentially on how well a given part of his empire got over the initial shock of its conquest by his armies. Put another way, it depended on how much time his officials had to repair the ravages of war and win the trust of those they administered. Broadly, they made some progress in the lands of the "inner empire", but they failed beyond them, in the areas Napoleon seized after about 1806.[64]

After Napoleon's defeat in 1815, the Congress of Vienna would restore Austria's territory, and under the leadership of Klemens Metternich, Austria (later Austria-Hungary) would become a key power in Central Europe. But the damage foreseen by Talleyrand-Perigord had been done, and tensions among the nationalities that made up the imperfectly mended empire would help bring about the World War of 1914–1918.

The Conquest of Germany

With Austria out of the way, Napoleon began to pressure the neutral (but nervous) Prussians. The Prussian king Frederick William III had signed a treaty with Czar Alexander of Russia. Alexander promised to ask England to give Prussia Hannover (the former British-ruled principality) and a subsidy for his army. In turn, Frederick promised to join Austria and Russia in the alliance against France.

After Napoleon won at Austerlitz, however, he was determined to smash the Third Coalition and particularly to extend the French Empire permanently into Germany. (At this time, "Germany" was, like "Italy," a geographical rather than a political term. It referred to the group of states east of the Rhine such as Bavaria, Prussia, and many smaller ones that made up the dying Holy Roman Empire.)

Napoleon took advantage of Prussia's weakness after Austerlitz, and forced the country to sign a treaty that "gave"

Hannover to France, badly straining Prussia's relations with Britain and Russia. Napoleon's goal seemed to be to turn Prussia into a satellite of the French Empire rather than attacking and occupying it directly.

On July 12, 1806, however, Napoleon made it clear that he wanted a permanent foothold in Germany. He established a grouping of small states called the Confederation of the Rhine, which he called his "family of kings." The new federation would receive a modern, efficient government on the French model. But the last straw for Prussia came when Napoleon turned around and offered Hannover back to Britain. On August 26 Prussia demanded that Napoleon withdraw all his troops to the west bank of the Rhine.

Instead, Napoleon advanced. On October 14 Napoleon's army attacked Prussian forces at Jena while Marshal Louis-Nicolas Davout moved on Auerstedt. The French won both battles. (Davout had the tougher fight, being outnumbered about two to one and having to hold on until reinforcements came.) Napoleon soon entered Berlin, the Prussian capital.

But Napoleon was not quite finished. He next moved into Poland, which had been partitioned between Austria and Prussia. With winter at hand, the French occupied Warsaw; Russian forces began to skirmish with them but soon retreated into their own territory, relatively unharmed. The Battle of Eylau, fought on February 8, 1807, was won mainly by the fierce winter: Both sides suffered heavy casualties and

Napoleon leads the French forces to victory over the Prussians during the battle at Jena on October 14, 1806. After his triumph, Napoleon captured the Prussian capital of Berlin.

Czar Alexander I embraces Napoleon during their meeting aboard a raft on the Niemen River. The meeting resulted in a cease-fire between the emperors and plans to conquer and divide Europe.

withdrew. The fighting continued on and off into mid-1807. On June 14 Marshal Lannes's corps approached the town of Friedland only to be met by Russian general Count Levin Bennigsen's entire army. Lannes fought desperately to hold on as Napoleon rushed reinforcements to him. The Russians had awkwardly straddled a bend in the Alle River. Napoleon's force of eighty thousand men then attacked, cutting off the Russians from escape and pushing many of them into the river or into the town where they surrendered.

Napoleon was at the height of his powers and his confidence. In less than three years Austria, Prussia, and Russia had been decisively defeated. In July 1807 he and Czar Alexander I arranged to meet on a raft moored in the middle of the Niemen River (a traditional boundary). The two emperors arranged to divide all of Europe between them, with Alexander allowing France to establish the Duchy of Warsaw (Poland). The Kingdom of Westphalia was carved out of Prussia to be given to Napoleon's brother Jerome. Perhaps equally significant, Alexander agreed to join the Continental System, a European trade boycott against Britain that had been declared by Napoleon in 1806.

A leading French author, François Auguste-René de Chateaubriand, foresaw the long-term effects of Napoleon's creation of the Confederation of the Rhine and his reorganization of many small German states. He wrote,

> Napoleon thought that by effacing [wiping out] so many frontiers and drawing all these strategic roads he was merely tracing the way from his barracks; in fact, he was opening the road to a fatherland.[65]

Historian James Harvey Robinson adds that Napoleon may have been the unwitting father of modern Germany:

> Napoleon, in a somewhat incidental and left-handed fashion, did so much to promote the progress both of democratic institutions and of nationality in Western Europe that he may, in a sense, be regarded as the putative father of them both . . . . He is the father of modern Germany.[66]

Following 1815, Napoleon's arrangement of German states was replaced by a German Confederation. While this fledgling national entity had the potential for a true united Germany, it became a political pawn for the emerging powers of Prussia and Austria. In 1870, however, Prussian leader Otto von Bismarck provoked France's Napoleon III to declare war. Bismarck used the conflict to unify Germany, defeating France, and creating the state that would loom so large over the first half of the twentieth century.

In 1807, however, Napoleon seemed to have Europe at his feet. But the footing was about to get treacherous, as he found himself embroiled in campaigns where the rules of war were very different even from the ones he had so brilliantly rewritten.

5 Changing the Rules: Unconventional War in Spain and Russia

Napoleon's new empire and its forced alliances extended from the Spanish border in the west to the Russian border in the east. Napoleon had gotten just about all of Europe, even Russia, to agree to abide by his Continental System, the trade boycott that he hoped would eventually cripple the meddlesome British. Only Portugal declined because it wanted to maintain good relations with Britain and, perhaps, because it doubted that Napoleon would march across Spain to threaten the small Atlantic kingdom.

Napoleon Invades Spain

Napoleon, however, quickly signed a treaty with Spain, wherein he promised his ally a piece of Portugal. French troops poured into Spain in October 1807, commanded by General Andoche Junot. They soon reached Lisbon, the Portuguese capital, and forced the royal family to flee across the Atlantic to Brazil. The "front door" of the continent had been shut to Britain.

During the invasion of Portugal, Napoleon had noticed that Spain was in temptingly bad shape. King Charles IV was weak, and the real power behind the

throne came from Manuel de Godoy, the queen's lover. Charles's son Ferdinand despised both his father and Godoy, and, for that reason, he had the support of most of the Spanish people. Not surprisingly, Ferdinand had his eye on the throne.

Spanish historian Rafael Altamira sums up the social and political situation in Spain at the time:

> An aristocracy, especially the courtiers, which had lost respect for the kings; rotten politics, ruled by personal animosities and reciprocal fears; absolute lack of patriotism among the upper classes, who subordinated everything else to passions and greed; the delirious hope of the masses, centered upon a Prince—Ferdinand—who had already shown himself to be both false and vengeful; and finally, the profound influence, in intellectual circles, of the ideas of the [Enlightenment] and the French Revolution.[67]

Evaluating the situation, Napoleon decided to have the troops that had invaded Portugal occupy the strong points of Spain, supposedly to defend that country from Britain. Meanwhile, he summoned the entire Spanish royal family to a meeting and separately convinced both Charles and Ferdinand that he would help them reach a public reconciliation (and allow them to live in comfort) if they "temporarily" gave him control of the throne by making him regent. Napoleon planned to keep the throne, of course, winning a bloodless victory and providing the Spanish with a liberal monarchy. According to J. Christopher Herold, however,

> the thought that the Spanish people might offer serious resistance never entered [Napoleon's] head. The Spanish royal family were corrupt fools, and he would trick them out of their kingdom; the Spanish people were a rabble that could be ignored.[68]

But on May 2, known thereafter as *Dos de Mayo*, the people of Madrid rose up and attacked Murat's French soldiers, resulting in hundreds killed on both sides. Napoleon instructed his officials to

> make the grandees and other influential persons of Spain thoroughly understand that the fate of Spain depends entirely on their behavior, that if Spain is aroused, and the safety of my troops compromised, the country will be dismembered.[69]

Napoleon then gave the throne to his brother Joseph. Ironically for someone whose career had been shaped by the popular forces of the French Revolution, Napoleon did not seem to understand that it was not the Spanish leaders who were stirring up the people, but the people spontaneously deciding, in many places and for many reasons, to resist.

One French general, Pierre-Antoine Dupont de l'Etang, was ordered to seize Cádiz. His force, like most of those Napoleon initially sent to Spain, was small and poorly trained. He defeated one Span-ish army only to have two more chase him as his supplies ran out and half the force deserted. Finally, left with only three thousand healthy soldiers, Dupont de l'Etang was trapped on the road to Bailén and surrendered. King Joseph panicked at the news and began to withdraw French forces north of the Ebro River. Napoleon scolded him:

> You should not be surprised at having to conquer your kingdom. Philip V and Henry IV had to conquer theirs. There is no question of dying, but of fighting and being victorious. I shall find in Spain the pillars of Hercules [that is, the farthest extent of Europe], not the limits of my power.[70]

Guerrilla Warfare

In June 1808 a small French army defeated a small Spanish force near the town of Saragossa, the capital of the Spanish province of Aragon. The Spanish commander retreated into the hills to try to recover before fighting again. Saragossa was left with only its civilian population to defend itself against the French.

The French commander demanded the town's surrender, and his heavy cavalry broke through the gates. What happened next was perhaps unprecedented in the history of warfare. Men, women, and even children fought the horsemen with improvised weapons. After nine hours of fighting the French lancers retreated in confusion from the city—an outcome not unlike the amazing resistance of the Jewish fighters in the Warsaw ghetto during World War II.

The French responded by laying siege to the town. The townspeople improvised fortifications while the French brought up artillery to bombard them. Despite the battering, the next French assault was resisted equally fiercely. At one place on the wall, the French attacked the gun crew of a Spanish cannon. A young woman who had just seen her husband killed ran to the cannon, plunged the burning match into the firing hole, shooting the cannon point-blank at the oncoming French, crying "*Viva España!*" The French retreated again. This heroic act would become a patriotic rallying point for the aroused Spanish people.

Defeats like that at Saragossa had discouraged Joseph; he wrote to Napoleon, "I am convinced that the new arrangements [the French conquest of Spain and Joseph's becoming king] will encounter more resistance in this country than Your Majesty might realize and that in the final analysis all this will bring happiness to no one." [71]

Napoleon's reaction was to send more troops; in November 1808 he took command of the armies, declaring, "I will conduct this war of peasants and monks myself and I hope to thrash the English soundly." [72] (This statement is revealing because it seems to focus on the English army in Portugal as the main foes and minimizes the role of the Spanish resistance.)

An Artist Portrays the Horrors of War

In Ten Against Napoleon, *Douglas Hilt describes how the Spanish artist Francisco de Goya portrayed the struggle against the French occupation.*

"Goya was moved by the heroism of both the Spanish military and common citizens. His etching of Agustina Zaragoza firing the cannon following the death of the crew acquired symbolic power; the individual assumes national grandeur. In [historian Gabriel] Lovett's words, 'She is Saragossa and Spain all in one, the symbol of Spanish resistance to Napoleon.'. . .

Goya was filled with revulsion at the wanton slaughter and human debasement, and hastened to depict the pillage and destruction in enduring form. The suppressed forces first envisaged in the Caprichos [etchings depicting dreamlike figures, hideously distorted] now stalked the land, unchecked and run amok. The etchings of the Demastres de la Guerra [Disasters of War], based on preliminary sketches made during his visit to Saragossa, portray the horror of total war shorn of any lingering false romanticism; the scenes of rape and other atrocities committed on and by civilians is an eloquent indictment of all wars for all time."

Napoleon's marshals fought a series of battles, defeating each Spanish army they encountered. French victories continued into 1809, and Saragossa was finally captured in February after a terrible siege.

In traditional battles, the Spanish proved to be no match for the French forces. In traditional war, when an army lost, it would surrender and negotiate the best terms it could with the victors. But the Spanish people did not play by these rules; they had invented a kind of war that would thereafter be known by the Spanish word *guerrilla*. Historian J. Christopher Herold describes the situation:

> While conventional warfare came to a standstill whenever the French forces gained temporary control, the guer-

rilla war continued with unabated violence until the complete expulsion of the French. It was fought with incredible cruelty on both sides. Every day French detachments were ambushed, supply trains raided, individual soldiers sniped at or knifed. Food might be poisoned; a friendly host, giving shelter to some tired courier, might turn out to be a guerrilla leader and murder him in his sleep; churches might be arsenals; priests might carry pistols concealed in their habits; accommodating wenches might turn into Judiths [a biblical heroine who killed an enemy warlord in his sleep].

The sense of constant danger and hatred created an almost psychotic state

"The Maid of Saragossa" helps staff a cannon crew during the defense of Spain. Her patriotic cry "Viva España" *inspired Spaniards to rise up against the French invaders.*

The French forces faced their greatest challenge in Spain, where guerrilla forces refused to be conquered.

of mind among the French. They were not content with the usual methods of reprisal—mass shootings of civilians taken arms in hand, burning of villages, confiscation of cattle, horses, and goods—but found release from their nervous tension in inflicting the most sadistic punishments and mutilations, in rape, in the desecration of churches, convents, and monasteries.[73]

The guerrilla forces were not centralized, but they were organized by juntas, or local groups of leaders. Some fought for nationalistic reasons, some were little more than bandit gangs. Brian Hammett notes that "in a large part of eastern and southern Spain the rebels fought as much against the [Spanish] nobility, secular or ecclesiastic, as against the French themselves. . . . Church and king were symbols not of conformity but of resistance."[74]

Others wanted to reform the monarchy or create a republic, ironically adopting the ideas of the French Revolution.

For example, the "Supreme Junta Central" issued this proclamation:

> Spaniards! The word "Fatherland" must no longer be an . . . empty word for you. In . . . your hearts it must signify the place where law and custom are inviolate, a place where talent is allowed to flourish and virtue is rewarded. Indeed, Spaniards, the day will soon dawn when the monarchy is given a solid and lasting foundation. . . . You will then possess basic rights which will hinder. . . . the growth of arbitrary power and foster law and order.[75]

These words combined all three appeals: to nation ("Fatherland"), to tradition ("law and custom"), and to the French ideas of equality and "basic rights."

A German veteran who served with the French forces would later recall the bewildering speed with which the guerrillas could strike and then vanish:

> As soon as an opportunity for a capture offered itself . . . the most active and daring among the people assembled and . . . rushed with the utmost rapidity upon their booty. . . . As soon as the enterprise was completed . . . [the members of the pickup fighting unit] quietly returned to their common occupations. . . . Thus, the communication on all roads was closed. Thousands of enemies were on the spot though not a single one could be discovered; no courier could be dispatched, without being taken; no supplies could be set off without being attacked; in short, no movement could be effected without being observed by a hundred eyes. At the same time, there existed no means of striking at . . . a combination

of this kind. The French . . . were obliged to be constantly on their guard against . . . the incessant molestations of an invisible enemy.[76]

In this new style of fighting, the superior firepower and accuracy of the trained French soldiers often did not help much. As one soldier recorded in his diary, after being attacked by guerrillas,

> we . . . held out for half an hour, everyone firing as much as he could. The cannon were hauled out, but the grapeshot . . . did not help . . . since the enemy formed a half-moon (curved) line and only a few could be hit, for they lay down on the ground behind the hedges . . . while every shot of theirs could hit our compressed column. Finally too many of our men fell, and . . . this hurried our retreat into the city.[77]

Wellington

As the French occupation of Spain bogged down in guerrilla warfare and sieges, the British saw an excellent opportunity. Lord Castlereagh, the British foreign secretary, ordered money sent to support the Spanish rebels. He also dispatched a small army under Arthur Wellesley, better known by his later title, the duke of Wellington.

Wellington had gained his military experience through hard fighting in the colonial wars in India. He had learned how to deal with a variety of local peoples, how to gather military intelligence, and how to improvise battlefield tactics. His performance had earned him the rank of major general in 1802.

In August 1808 Wellington's forces landed in Portugal. When French general Junot attacked them, Wellington won the battle but his superior officers refused to let him pursue and destroy the enemy. Instead, they allowed the French to sail peacefully back to France. This lost opportunity led to a court-martial for Wellington and his superiors, but Wellington was exonerated.

In April 1809 Wellington returned to Portugal and began two years of tough campaigning. He mainly fought on the defensive, preserving his army while helping coordinate the efforts of the Spanish guerrilla forces.

By 1812 Napoleon's attention had shifted to Russia, leaving Wellington and the "second string" French armies to fight back and forth over the Spanish peninsula. Finally, toward the end of 1813, Wellington began the campaign that decisively defeated Marshal Nicolas-Jean Soult, who surrendered when he heard of Napoleon's own downfall.

Looking back from exile, Napoleon later admitted:

> I started off on the wrong foot in this whole [Spanish] business. Its immorality must have seemed too patent [obvious], its injustice too cynical; the whole thing remains ugly, since I lost out. For, having failed, my attempt is revealed in its hideous nakedness, stripped of all grandeur and of the many beneficial reforms I contemplated.[78]

The legal and political reforms that Napoleon established in conquered areas could not be implemented in unconquered Spain. But as in Italy and Germany, the French ideas of liberal reform

Portuguese forces under English commander Arthur Wellesley, the duke of Wellington, defeat the French during the 1812 battle of Ciudad Rodrigo.

of institutions would be used to eventually reform Spain. Looking toward the future, one reformer declared:

> The Spaniards are fighting to be free. And, for those . . . objectives to be achieved, is it enough for them to . . . face death with serenity and exterminate the French? Assuming that the latter are expelled . . . if we did not establish a system of . . . just, wise, and beneficent laws, if we did not banish from amongst ourselves the multitude of errors . . . that have reduced us to the level of animals, if we did not augment the nation's wealth by diminishing the unproductive classes . . . would we be able to . . . feel ourselves safe from . . . the usurper, or any of the power that sought to impose a tyranny upon us?[79]

Following the defeat of Napoleon, a conservative monarchy would be restored under a king, Ferdinand VII, who had in-

---

British Defenders in Spain

In David Gates's The Spanish Ulcer, *French general Thomas Bugeaud recalls how the French assault on a British position fell apart.*

"The usual artillery action first took place. Soon, in great haste, without studying the position, without taking time to examine whether there were means to make a flank attack, we marched straight on, taking the bull by the horns. About 1000 yards from the English line the men became excited, called out to one another, and hastened their march; the column began to become a little confused. The English remained quite silent with ordered arms, and from their readiness appeared to be a long red wall.

This steadiness invariably produced an effect on our young soldiers. Very soon we got nearer, crying 'Vive l'Empereur! En Avant!' [Long live the Emperor! Forward!] . . . The English line remained silent, still, and immovable, with ordered arms, even when we were only 300 yards distant, and it appeared to ignore the storm about to break. . . . At this moment of intense excitement, the English wall shouldered arms; an indescribable feeling would root many of our men to the spot; they began to fire. The enemy's steady, concentrated volleys swept our ranks; decimated, we turned round seeking to recover our equilibrium; then three deafening cheers broke the silence of our opponents; at the third they were on us, pushing our disorganized flight."

---

deed succeeded his father, Charles IV. The struggle for reform during the rest of the century would be painfully slow and inconclusive.

The Czar and the Emperor

In July 1807, far across the continent in the Prussian city of Tilsit (in present-day Lithuania), the victorious Napoleon and powerful Czar Alexander of Russia had apparently settled the future of Europe. Alexander had a curious emotional relationship with Napoleon, who had dazzled him in their earlier meetings. Alexander initially seemed to admire Napoleon. Perhaps Napoleon's achievements encouraged Alexander to seek a more splendid, imperial role for himself and for Russia.

In 1808 the two rulers met at Erfurt, another Prussian city. Napoleon, who had created some new German states, was there to preside over the crowning of their kings. Alexander had been invited because Napoleon wanted to secure the Russian's help in stopping any new attacks from Austria. The French dictator was taking this precaution because he was about to leave for Spain to deal with the problem that he referred to as "the Spanish ulcer"—the defiant Spanish population his brother was unable to subdue. Napoleon seemed confident that he could charm Alexander out of almost anything, but the Russian emperor became increasingly suspicious.

When Napoleon had his marriage to Joséphine annulled on trumped-up religious grounds, Alexander's apprehension grew. For he knew Napoleon's real reason for dissolving the marriage—that Joséphine had failed to provide him with a son—and

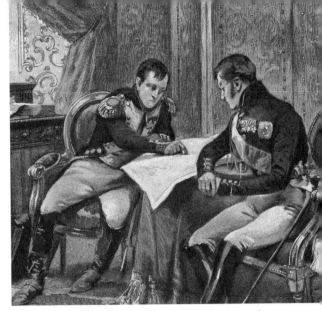

Napoleon and Czar Alexander pore over a map of Europe during their 1807 meeting in Tilsit, determining the fate of the continent.

Alexander feared Napoleon's impending marriage to the young Austrian archduchess Marie-Louise meant that a French-Austrian alliance against Russia was in the offing. Moreover, Alexander had begun to regret having allowed Napoleon to establish the Duchy of Warsaw, which was beginning to look like a wedge for potential use against Russia.

Napoleon, in turn, had become frustrated by Russia's abandonment of the European trade boycott he had organized, the Continental System. Indeed, the czar had even gone so far as to put a luxury tax on French goods.

Napoleon was now facing a changing Russia. The traditional Russian love of the motherland was being supplemented by a growing sense of national identity. During the eighteenth century, under strong leaders such as the reformer Peter the Great, Russia had expanded toward central Europe (Poland), the Baltic and Black Seas, and Scandinavia. Russia had begun to

Napoleon marries Marie-Louise, archduchess of Austria. The French-Austrian alliance greatly worried Russia's Czar Alexander.

think of itself as a major European power even while its social structure was still feudal, with a serf-holding nobility and an economy that remained primitive by western European standards.

Napoleon Invades Russia

In 1812 Napoleon decided to invade Russia, hoping to make Alexander a more cooperative subordinate rather than a would-be equal. He did this despite a warning from the Czar, passed through French ambassador Armand-Augustin-Louis de Caulaincourt:

If the Emperor makes war on me, it is possible, even probable, that we shall be defeated, assuming that we fight. But that will not mean that he can dictate a peace. The Spaniards have often been defeated; and they are not beaten, nor have they submitted. But they are not so far away from Paris as we are, and have neither our climate nor our resources to help them. We shall take no risks.[80]

On June 24, 1812, the Grande Armée crossed the Russian frontier on the Niemen River at Kovno (Kaunas, in present-day Lithuania). This force differed from Napoleon's original army that had won his victories in Germany a few years earlier. The new army was much larger and more diverse, with 600,000 men (about 510,000 infantry and 90,000 cavalry and horse artillery) from 20 nationalities (even the tiny principality of San Marino sent a handful of soldiers). Austria and Prussia, forced into alliance by Napoleon's victories in Germany, contributed substantial army divisions.

Napoleon realized that this vast and cumbersome army could not "live off the land" the way smaller ones had in the German campaign. In fact, the army needed 200,000 horses and cattle to pull 25,000 wagons and artillery (1,250 field guns) and to carry the cavalry into battle. "I have never made greater preparations,"[81] Napoleon assured Marshal Davout. But as they set out they "formed the largest traffic jam in European history"[82] according to Alan Schom.

Napoleon believed the Russians would have to take notice of his huge force. If they did not stand and give battle before too much of Russia had been overrun, they might launch their own offensive toward Warsaw. In either case, Napoleon planned a massive flanking maneuver that would bring him behind the Russians, cutting them off and hopefully surrounding them.

Napoleon's juggernaut streamed east from Kovno toward Vilna. The two main Russian generals, Mikhail Barclay de Tolly and Pyotr Bagration argued at first whether to retreat into the Russian interior or to attack toward Warsaw (one of the two possibilities Napoleon had foreseen). Finally, Barclay de Tolly ordered a retreat.

Murat's French cavalry approached Vilna and Jerome Bonaparte's force approached Grodno, crossing the Niemen and Bug Rivers. But other than some annoying skirmishes with fast-riding Cossacks, there was a remarkable lack of Russians in the area. The Grande Armée, some of whose soldiers had marched all the way from Spain, began to tire in the hot summer weather. By July the weather changed to cold and rain and sickness began to spread among both men and horses. As the army crossed the rivers and spread out, the food distribution system also broke down. One Bavarian corps was ordered to "Let each man take wherever he can find it, and live as well or as badly as he can manage it."[83]

Meanwhile, the two main Russian armies under Bagration and Barclay de Tolly continued to retreat while the French corps probed ahead, trying to locate them. Davout was ordered to advance toward Minsk to try to push Bagration's army to the south and trap it against Davout's and Jerome's corps. Two other marshals, Murat and Michel Ney, were ordered to try to nail down Barclay de Tolly's army. Napoleon would hold the reserves (including his very powerful Imperial

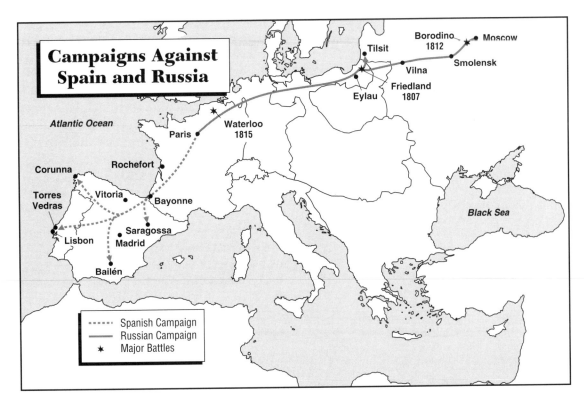

Campaigns Against Spain and Russia

Atlantic Ocean

Paris

Waterloo 1815

Corunna

Rochefort

Torres Vedras

Vitoria

Bayonne

Lisbon

Saragossa

Madrid

Bailén

Tilsit

Borodino 1812

Moscow

Vilna

Smolensk

Eylau

Friedland 1807

Black Sea

- - - - - Spanish Campaign
───── Russian Campaign
★ Major Battles

Guard), ready to send them to cut off any Russian force that escaped the huge envelopment. But when Davout and Jerome quarreled over who would lead their forces, Bagration escaped and yet a third Russian army began to move into Poland.

According to Caulaincourt, when Napoleon had entered the city of Vitebsk, where he had hoped to trap Barclay de Tolly's army,

> [Napoleon] was dismayed by the departure of the inhabitants of the city and by the flight of the troops into the countryside. This system of retreat perhaps finally opened his eyes to the eventual consequences that such a war as this could have on us, a strategy that was daily drawing us farther and farther from France. But then with the slightest hope in our favor again he cast aside such practical considerations and their consequences, his hope once again unrealistically rekindled [for a fast victory].[84]

In fact, the two Russian forces had both escaped Napoleon's traps, and their retreats converged on Smolensk. Napoleon directed the weakened but still large Grande Armée to that city, which was taken under bombardment and entered on August 16. But rather than standing to fight, the Russians, both soldiers and civilians, retreated again from the burning city. Barclay de Tolly's rear guard kept the pursuing French at bay, frustrating Napoleon yet again. As one observer had noted: "No troops can and do defend ground better in retreat than the Russians. Their artillery is so well horsed, so nimbly and so handily worked, that it bowls over almost all irregularities of surface with ease, lightness and velocity that give it great superiority."[85]

What was Napoleon to do now? Smolensk was too small to serve as a base, and muddy fall would soon turn to freezing winter. Napoleon wrote to the czar telling him that there should be no hard feelings, there was nothing personal about this war, and surely a settlement could be reached. The czar's response was silence.

By now the main French army was down to 145,000 men, a quarter of its original size. Finally, however, the blows to Russian pride as city after city fell began to have their effect. As Napoleon headed toward Moscow, Alexander resolved to defend the capital, choosing the popular General Kutuzov to take command.

A Hollow Victory

On September 6 the French army, now reduced to 130,000, encountered the Russian army's position in the hills near the town of Borodino on the road to Moscow. Although Napoleon proclaimed his confidence in the outcome of the coming battle, inwardly he was suffering from doubts about victory, depression, and increasingly troublesome stomach and bowel disorders.

Napoleon sketched out the lines of attack for his marshals, hoping that his superior artillery of six hundred guns and the sudden shock of the assault would crack open the Russian defenses. But the emperor was not his usual self. Instead of actively managing the battle and using his sense of timing to orchestrate the attack, he stayed inside his command post, a bad cold adding to his woes. Without Napoleon's personal leadership, the marshals' attacks were poorly coordinated. The battle became an attempt to batter

Russian forces clash with the French at Borodino. The battle had no clear victor, but the Russians eventually retreated and the French continued on to Moscow.

the Russians head-on, but the entrenched defense always has a major advantage in such fights.

As the afternoon wore on, Marshals Murat, Davout, and Ney repeatedly begged Napoleon to order the Imperial Guard, always held in reserve, to add their weight to the attack. As usual, Napoleon refused. While the guard might have broken the Russians' back, Napoleon had become acutely conscious of how far he was from France and felt that he could not afford to risk his one remaining reserve.

The battle at Borodino had no real winner although both sides claimed victory. The two sides together lost seventy thousand men. Kutuzov retreated, and Napoleon was able to continue down the road and enter Moscow on September 14.

The city was virtually deserted. The French trudged up to the Kremlin, the ancient Russian palace of the czars. There was no one to offer surrender. According to the traditional rules of war, when one king occupied an enemy's capital, the conquered monarch presented himself for peace talks, wherein he agreed to most if not all of the victor's demands. But Alexander was not present, and he did not reply to any of Napoleon's messages. The absence of a treaty partner posed a serious problem for Napoleon, who after all, did not want to conquer and occupy Russia, an impossible task. Rather, he wanted Alexander to cooperate obediently in his larger plans for Europe.

Meanwhile, fires began springing up mysteriously around the city. Napoleon,

Napoleon and his staff enter the Russian capital of Moscow. Not only did the invaders find the city deserted, they also discovered that the czar was absent and refused to present himself for negotiations.

Governor Fyodor Rostopchin had ordered the evacuation of the city's inhabitants into the countryside, had released jail inmates to roam the streets—and he had even destroyed the city's fire fighting equipment!

For the next month, Napoleon was torn between staying in Moscow until the czar was willing to talk or retreating back to a place where the army could get supplies and build shelters for the winter that was so soon to come. While holding back from a battle, General Kutuzov encouraged partisan raiders to harass the French supplies and communications. Caulaincourt warned Napoleon:

> We are already in great jeopardy, our shortage of supplies, of transport ani-

A frustrated Napoleon watches as Moscow is engulfed in flames to prevent the French from sacking the capital.

whose career had begun with the burning battleships at Toulon, now saw what he would later describe as

> mountains of red, rolling flames like immense waves of the sea, alternately bursting forth and lifting themselves to skies of fire, then sinking into the ocean of flames below. Oh, it was the most grand, the most sublime, and the most terrifying sight the world ever beheld![86]

Unknown to Napoleon, General Kutuzov had decided not to save Moscow. And

Napoleon Stirs His Troops

"On the 7th, at two in the morning, the emperor was surrounded by the marshals in the position taken the evening before. At half past five o'clock the sun rose without clouds: it had rained the previous evening.

'This is the sun of Austerlitz,' said the emperor. Though but the month of September, it was as cold as a December in Moravia. The army received the omen; the drum beat, and the following order of the day was read: 'Soldiers! behold the field of battle you have so much desired! henceforth victory depends on you; it is necessary to us; it will give us plenty, good quarters [housing] for the winter, and a speedy return to your country. Behave yourself as you did at Austerlitz, at Friedland, at Witepsk, and at Smolensko; and that the latest posterity may speak of your conduct this day with pride, that it may say of you, He was at the great battle under the walls of Moscow.' The army answered with [repeated applause]. The ground on which the army stood was spread with the dead bodies of the Russians killed the preceding day."

mals for our artillery, our great number of ill and wounded, the lack of proper winter clothing for our troops. Everyone needs a sheepskin coat, fur-lined gloves, heavy hats, stockings, and thick winter boots against the ice and snow. We lack everything. Our smiths don't even have the proper heavy horseshoes used here [in winter]. How can teams of horses be expected to haul our artillery across ice? And then there is the question of our lines of communications. It is still unseasonably warm now, but what will it be in two week's time when winter sets in?[87]

Retreat from Moscow

Finally, in October 1812, Napoleon decided to abandon Moscow. He planned to move southward through the cities of Kaluga and Bryansk rather than back along his original route. He hoped that would allow him to gather fresh supplies, especially forage for the remaining horses and then establish winter quarters somewhere near Smolensk and Minsk. (This would also allow him to save face by claiming that this movement into new territory was an additional attack, not a retreat.)

Kutuzov blocked the route, however; the French and Russians fought back and forth over the town of Maloyaroslavets, about seventy miles southwest of Moscow, while a band of Cossacks nearly captured Napoleon himself. Napoleon then ordered that the army retreat along the original route of advance and head for Smolensk.

As Russian raiders nipped at their heels and destroyed supply depots, the French army stumbled along. The Cos-

sacks were particularly troublesome. One observer described a typical rider:

Mounted on a very little, ill-conditioned, but well-bred horse, which can walk at the rate of five miles per hour with ease, or, in his speed, dispute the race with the swiftest—with a short whip on his wrist (as he wears no spur)—armed with a lance, a pistol in his girdle, and a sword, he never fears a competitor in single combat. [Cos-

Death March: The Retreat from Moscow

In his memoirs, French sergeant Bourgogne recalls the horrors of the retreat from Moscow across Russia's winter landscape.

"We walked on, thinking of all that had passed, stumbling over dead and dying men. The cold was even more intense than the day before. We joined two men in the line who had their teeth in a bit of horseflesh. They said, if they waited any longer, it would be frozen too hard to eat. They assured us as a fact that they had seen foreign soldiers (Croats) of our army dragging corpses out of the fire, cutting them up and eating them. I never saw this sort of thing myself, but I believe it frequently happened during this fatal campaign. . . . I am sure if I had not found any horseflesh myself, I could have turned cannibal. To understand this situation, one must have felt the madness of hunger; failing a man to eat, one could have demolished the devil himself, if he were only cooked."

French soldiers wearily march through the snow during their retreat from Moscow. As starvation set in, some soldiers resorted to cannibalizing the dead.

Decimated by cold and hunger, a column of French soldiers crosses the Berezina River after leaving Moscow.

sacks] . . . attack in dispersion, and when they do reunite to charge, it is not with a systematic formation but en masse . . . the swarm attack.[88]

The heavy snows began in November. Horses died in droves, and men froze and died by the side of the road. When they finally reached Smolensk, the French found few supplies, and Napoleon ordered them to march on. Kutuzov's forces then moved in for the kill. With the French army down to only forty thousand men and facing eighty thousand, Marshal Ney's rear guard nevertheless attacked the Russians. When that failed, Ney made a daring march cross-country around the Russians and the thousand survivors rejoined Napoleon's main force.

Finally, on November 26, the tattered remnant of the Grande Armée crossed the icy Berezina River on pontoon bridges hastily thrown up by French engineers. Leaving the army to trudge back through Poland, Napoleon made the speediest possible return to Paris, where news of defeat had encouraged plotters to try to over-throw the government. Napoleon's most ambitious campaign had ended in failure. Napoleon would later make excuses:

Was I defeated by the efforts of the Russians? No! My failure must be attributed to pure accident, to absolute fatality. First a capital [Moscow] was burnt to the ground, in spite of its inhabitants and through foreign intrigues; then winter set in with such unusual suddenness and severity that it was regarded as a kind of phenomenon. To these disasters must be added a mass of false reports, silly intrigues, treachery, stupidity, and in short, many things that will perhaps one day come to light.[89]

The hindsight of history suggests, however, that Napoleon's strategy, designed brilliantly to cut off and destroy armies, was not effective against a Russia that could use time, space, and weather to wear down the invader. Much the same thing would happen in 1942 when Hitler's armies invaded Soviet Russia.

6 Defeating Napoleon: The European War of Liberation

As the year 1813 began, Napoleon's empire was rapidly coming apart. As he would tell Austrian minister Klemens Metternich later in the year, "Your sovereigns born on the throne can let themselves be beaten twenty times and still return to their capitals. My domination will not survive the day when I cease to be strong and therefore feared."[90]

Austria and Prussia had been bound to him only by fear; with the Grande Armée destroyed in Russia, leaders throughout Germany began to realize that they might be able to defeat Napoleon once and for all. They looked at what had happened in Spain, in Russia, and even in Germany itself, where Archduke Charles of Austria had withstood and beaten back Napoleon at the battles of Aspern and Essling in 1809. A couple of years earlier, Napoleon's brother Jerome had warned that

> if war breaks out, all the countries between the Rhine and the Oder will rise as one man. The cause of unrest is not simply a strong impatience with a foreign yoke; it lies deeper in the ruin that faces every class of people, the crushing taxation; the war levies, the billeting [forced housing] of troops; all the military coming and going; and a constant series of harassments.[91]

Now the prediction was coming true. Returning to Paris, Napoleon desperately tried to shore up his power and drafted more soldiers, mostly inexperienced youths, rebuilding his army to about two hundred thousand men. The army, however, had a critical shortage of horses for cavalry and artillery.

The War of Liberation

In March Prussia allied itself to Russia and declared war on France. Prussia had reformed and reorganized its armies over the past few years, finally learning from the innovations of revolutionary France. As thoughtful Prince Friedrich von Hardenburg had observed during the earlier German campaigns,

> the French Revolution, of which the current wars are an extension, has brought the French people a wholly new vigor, despite all their turmoil and bloodshed. . . . It is an illusion to think that we can resist the Revolution effectively by clinging more closely to the old order. . . . Thus our objective, our guiding principle, must be a revolution in the better sense, a revolution leading di-

Napoleon's Empire, 1799–1812

United Kingdom of Great Britain and Ireland
North Sea
London
English Channel
Atlantic Ocean
Bay of Biscay
FRANCE
Paris
SWITZERLAND
PORTUGAL
SPAIN
Madrid
NORWAY
SWEDEN
Stockholm
DENMARK
Berlin
CONFEDERATION OF THE RHINE 1806
Warsaw
GRAND DUCHY OF WARSAW
AUSTRIA
Vienna
ITALY
Elba
Corsica
PAPAL STATES
Rome
Naples
Sardinia
Tyrrhenian Sea
Sicily
Adriatic Sea
Moscow
RUSSIA
Black Sea
OTTOMAN EMPIRE
Constantinople
Aegean Sea
Cyprus
Crete
Mediterranean Sea
Alexandria
EGYPT
Cairo

France, 1799

Under French Rule by 1812

Allied with France in 1812

rectly to the great goal, the elevation of humanity through the wisdom of those in authority and not through a violent impulsion from within or without.[92]

Napoleon's new army met the allies at Lützen, winning a partial victory; but he lacked enough cavalry to pursue the enemy, following standard military tactics. Napoleon then crossed the river at Dresden, threatening to advance on the Prussian capital of Berlin. The Prussians and Russians disagreed about whether to defend or withdraw. Taking advantage of the confusion, Napoleon attacked the allies at Bautzen on May 20–21. By combining a frontal assault and a flank attack, he drove the allies out of their positions. Again, however, lack of cavalry prevented a decisive result.

Stung by the defeats, the allies offered a seven-week cease fire, which Napoleon accepted. Napoleon had decided that he could not win without cavalry reinforcements, and he was worried about Austria joining the war against him.

Actually, Austria's Metternich did not want to destroy France because he feared the advance of Russia into central Europe. Rather, Metternich was trying to get Napoleon to agree to withdraw his troops behind the natural boundaries of the French Pyrenees and the Rhine River. He wanted a Europe where a "balance of power" would prevent any one monarch from becoming too powerful.

Prussia, on the other hand, was eager to pursue what became known as the German War of Liberation, with the goal of destroying Napoleon for good. Meanwhile,

Diplomatic Disaster

According to Jeremy Black's article "Napoleon's Impact on International Relations" in History Today, *Napoleon might have been able to salvage part of his empire if he had been willing to compromise.*

"In 1813 Napoleon succeeded in uniting Austria, Britain, Prussia, Russia and Sweden in an attack on him. Both then and in 1814 he failed to offer terms that would divide his assailants, despite the fact that Austria distrusted Russia and would have liked to have retained a strong France, while the Russians sought a strong France in order to balance Britain. Their definitions of strength included a France territorially more extensive than in 1789 and, at least initially, they were willing to accept a continuance of Napoleon's rule, but his instinctive refusal to accept limits or half measures wrecked such schemes."

an ambassador from London arrived with money to pay for the allied armies. In addition, Prince Bernadotte of Sweden, a former marshal of Napoleon, marched his army of forty thousand into the field near Berlin, hoping for the chance to usurp the French throne.

By August Austria, too, had joined the allies. Occupying the town of Dresden on August 26–27, Napoleon and his 70,000 soldiers faced a combined Austrian, Prussian, and Russian force of about 150,000. Seeing that a ravine separated the left wing of the allies from the rest of their army, Napoleon attacked and separated the left, then successfully defeated the center and right. But again, the victory was not decisive.

By October both sides had gathered reinforcements, though it was clear that the allied forces were getting larger faster. Near Leipzig, a maze of five rivers or streams and a neighboring marsh became the ground for the Battle of Leipzig (also called the Battle of the Nations because of the presence of so many major European powers).

The battle was an indecisive battering. Napoleon's marshals were perhaps more preoccupied with their personal future than what was rapidly appearing to be Napoleon's lost cause. The troops were inexperienced, the ammunition was low, and the plans were uninspired. Napoleon retreated from the battlefield in good order, but the allies had won a strategic victory and moved inexorably toward Paris.

Napoleon refused to give up and grimly decided to defend Paris, but he now had only 120,000 troops against more than 600,000 on the allied side. Rather than coordinate their attacks, the allied armies operated independently, attacking through Switzerland, across the Rhine, the Netherlands, and Italy. (The duke of Wellington, having driven the remaining French forces out of Spain, now moved up into southern France.)

Napoleon fought desperately against one army, then another, winning minor victories but seeing his forces melting away. The French people began to make it clear that they had had enough. Marshal Murat went over to the allies, and Talleyrand-Perigord saw the advantage of negotiating with the enemy for the removal of Napoleon and the restoration of the Bourbon monarchy.

Finally, the French Senate, which had seldom opposed the emperor even on the smallest matter, declared Napoleon deposed and the monarchy restored. Under the Treaty of Fontainebleau, signed on April 11, 1814, the exiled Napoleon was given the little island of Elba (near his birthplace of Corsica) as a miniature kingdom, together with an annual income of two million francs.

Napoleon was finished. Or was he?

The Congress of Vienna

Following Napoleon's defeat, European leaders organized a unique meeting called the Congress of Vienna. As historian Paul Johnson notes,

Vienna was the first modern peace conference: an attempt not only to settle all outstanding matters throughout

The allies pound Napoleon's forces during the Battle of Leipzig. Although the battle was indecisive, the allies gained the upper hand.

Europe and to have decisions reached endorsed by all its states, but to draw up, as it were, a constitution for the entire European community as a means to underwrite international law and so preserve peace on a permanent basis.[93]

The meeting was a splendid affair and became known as the "Dancing Congress" because of the lavish nightly balls and parties that took place after the meetings. However, without the threat of Napoleon, the leaders and diplomats had no reason to unite and were soon quarreling over the division of Europe. Czar Alexander wanted the return of territories in Poland.

Britain's Castlereagh wanted to set up a balance of power where a strong Austria and Prussia would prevent either Russia or a revived France from overrunning Europe. The Austrians and Prussians, too, had their separate agendas.

This seeming deadlock gave the wily Talleyrand-Perigord the opportunity to insert defeated France into the negotiations. He reminded some of the participants of the dangers their countries faced now that Napoleon was no longer present to neutralize or threaten certain other participants. As a result, Britain, Austria, and France agreed to support each other if attacked by Russia or Prussia.

Preparing for exile, Napoleon bids farewell to his Imperial Guard at Fontainebleau in April 1814. Napoleon spent his exile on the island of Elba, where he frantically planned his return to politics.

The "Hundred Days"

The news then came that Napoleon had returned to France. As part of the face-saving arrangement, Napoleon had been allowed a small army of about a thousand men to protect Elba, and he had the use of several ships. He had been closely monitoring the situation in France, where the new Bourbon king, Louis XVIII, was particularly unpopular among the many peasants who feared their land might be restored to the old nobility as well as among revolutionary citizens who still supported the ideals of the republic.

When Napoleon heard a rumor that his former police minister, Joseph Fouché, was about to launch a coup against the king, he decided it was time to roll the dice once more. Setting sail on February 26, 1815, Napoleon and his tiny army eluded the British patrols around the island, reaching the French coast. Napoleon then issued the following bulletin: "Soldiers! In my exile I heard your voice! . . . Your general, called to the throne by the voice of the people and raised on your shields, is restored to you: come and join him."[94]

The audacity of Napoleon's gamble was breathtaking. He would have to travel hundreds of miles to Paris without being captured by the king, who (theoretically at least) had hundreds of thousands of soldiers at his disposal. At Cannes, Napoleon jauntily proclaimed, "I am the sovereign of the Island of Elba, and have come with six hundred men to attack the King of France and his six hundred thousand soldiers. I shall conquer this kingdom."[95]

The authorities were slow to react, and a considerable number of French citizens still regarded their former emperor

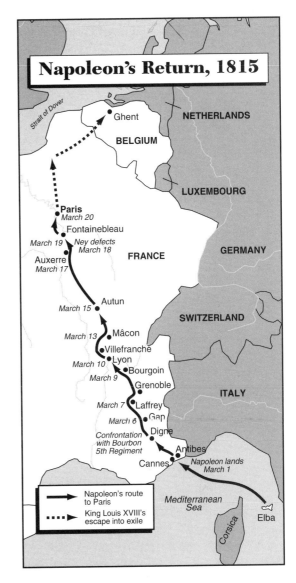

with affection or longed for the old glory days. Alan Schom describes what happened when Napoleon's party reached Grenoble and the garrison troops came out to arrest him:

"Soldiers of the 5th Infantry Battalion, I am your Emperor. If there is anyone among you who wishes to kill his emperor, here I am," he said defiantly

The Fickle French Press

In Waterloo, *David Chandler quotes a series of headlines in French news sheets that became more flattering as Napoleon got closer to Paris.*

The Tiger has broken out of his cage.
The Ogre has been three days at sea.
The Wretch has landed at Fréjus.
The Buzzard has reached Antibes.
The Invader has arrived at Grenoble.
The General has entered Lyons.
Napoleon slept at Fontainebleau last night.
The Emperor will proceed to the Tuileries today.
His Imperial Majesty will address his loyal subjects
     tomorrow!

holding his coat open for them to fire at his heart. Although one captain did order the men to fire, nothing happened, and suddenly there was a thundering spontaneous outburst—"Vive l'Empereur!"—as hundreds of men threw down their weapons and broke ranks. They rushed over to Napoleon, knelt before him, and kissed the hem of his winter coat, even his sword.[96]

By the time Napoleon reached Paris on March 20, Marshal Ney and his troops had gone over to him. The new king and his government panicked and fled. Napoleon feverishly set about creating a new Grande Armée to meet the attack he knew would come. To gain support, he used carefully crafted propaganda to reinvent himself as the savior of French liberty:

I wish to be less the sovereign of France and more the first of her citizens. I am a product of the Revolution . . . [and]

have come to free the French people from the enslavement in which the priests and nobles wanted to entrap them.[97]

For their part, the leaders and diplomats at Vienna did not underestimate the threat of a resurgent Napoleon. They proclaimed that,

in breaking the Convention which established him in the Isle of Elba, Bonaparte is destroying the sole legal title to which his existence is attached. In reappearing in France with projects of troubles and upsettings, he has deprived himself of the protection of the laws, and has manifested in the face of the universe that it cannot have peace or truce with him. In consequence The Powers declare, that Napoleon Bonaparte is placed outside civil and social relations, and that as an enemy and disturber of the peace of the world, he has delivered himself over to public prosecution.[98]

92 ■ THE AGE OF NAPOLEON

In other words, Napoleon was not to be treated as a fellow king with whom one played the game of war, swapping territories and shifting advantages. He was to be treated as an outlaw.

The Last Campaign

The allies formed the Seventh Coalition. Britain would provide 5 million pounds in cash and an army under the duke of Wellington, the victor in Spain. Marshal Gebhard von Blücher's Prussian army and an army under Karl Philipp zu Schwarzenberg of Austria would also converge on France, heading for Paris. There were no elaborate strategic plans: They were relying on the likelihood that they would have twice as many soldiers as the French and the assumption that Napoleon's hastily assembled forces would be poorly equipped.

Napoleon knew that time was his enemy. He was already substantially outnumbered, and every month that passed would increase allied superiority. As Wellington and Blücher maneuvered their forces in Belgium and prepared to enter France, Napoleon relied on the strategy that had served him so well during his early career in Italy.

In mid-June, Wellington's force was still scattered and Blücher was some distance away. Napoleon decided to try to drive his army between the two allied

Prussian marshal Blücher is unhorsed at Ligny while battling Napoleon's army. Napoleon forced the Prussians to flee, leaving Blücher wounded and desperately needing to regroup.

armies, seizing the road to Brussels and preventing the allies from joining. He could then attack the allied armies separately at favorable odds. Napoleon prepared to send Marshal Ney's force toward the town of Quatre Bras on the way to Brussels.

Napoleon had planned to first hit the straggling Wellington, but when Marshal Emmanuel de Grouchy's cavalry scouts reported sighting Blücher's Prussians, Napoleon decided to attack them instead to prevent them from reaching Wellington. Blücher decided to stand and fight at the town of Ligny, holding until Wellington could join him.

On June 16 the fierce fight swayed back and forth, with Blücher's lines stretching. Observing that the center was weakening, Napoleon ordered Ney at Quatre Bras to go around the Prussians' right flank, hoping that together he and his old comrade could envelop and destroy Blücher's army. But Ney seemed confused and unable to follow Napoleon's orders for a vigorous attack. Finally Wellington arrived at Quatre Bras, and Ney, occupied with that new threat, could not complete the destruction of the Prussian army.

Meanwhile, as Napoleon prepared to punch through the center of Blücher's line, a lost French corps suddenly appeared near Napoleon's left flank. By the time Napoleon had determined the identity of the unknown army, Blücher had counterattacked. But with Wellington much farther away than Blücher had realized, the Prussians could no longer stand, and Napoleon drove them from the field with Blücher badly wounded.

The next morning Napoleon received reports that most of the Prussian forces had fled. Sending Grouchy to pursue them, Napoleon turned his attention to Wellington. But Grouchy's pursuit was not vigorous, and the French lost contact with the Prussians.

Waterloo

The duke of Wellington had earned a reputation as one of the few commanders who could stand up to Napoleon. But when Marshal Soult had suggested that Napoleon keep Grouchy's force for use against the British general, Napoleon had sneered: "Because you have been beaten by Wellington, you think him a great general. I tell you that Wellington is a bad general, and that this will be a picnic."[99]

On Sunday, June 18, three armies were preparing to do battle in the rolling hills and patches of woods near the village of Waterloo, south of Brussels. Wellington applied all the knowledge of defensive warfare he had acquired during his years in the hills of Spain. In particular, he positioned many of his lines on the other side of the slopes away from the French. This protected them from cannon fire and concealed them from attacking French columns, yet it also allowed the British to suddenly step up and deliver devastating musket volleys.

French marshal Honoré Reille forewarned Napoleon of Wellington's advantage:

> Well-posted [positioned] as Wellington knows how to post them and attacked head-on, I consider the English infantry to be impregnable in view of its calm tenacity and superior firepower. Before we can reach them with the bayonet, half our attacking force

Napoleon leads a fatigued column of soldiers. Despite his unfavorable odds at Waterloo, the brash commander refused to retreat.

would be shot down. But the English army is less agile, less supple, less maneuverable than ours. If we cannot conquer it with a head-on attack, we could do so by maneuvering.[100]

While the French attack developed, Wellington later recalled, Napoleon "did not maneuver at all. He just moved forward in the old style."[101] The attack did not commence until noon because Napoleon was waiting for the ground to dry from the overnight rains.

Although the main French objective was the commanding heights of Mount St. Jean, the French attack soon became entangled in a fierce fight over the Château de Goumont. Meanwhile, Napoleon dis-

covered that Blücher, far from having fled, had gotten around Grouchy, resolutely marched his tired troops through the night, and would soon arrive at the battlefield. This would change an evenly matched battle (72,000 French versus 68,000 allied) to a much more difficult contest. Still, Napoleon decided that he could not retreat and wait for more favorable odds. Schwarzenberg's army of 250,000 was on the way to Paris after all.

Napoleon now sent in the main attack up the hill toward a strongpoint in a farm called La Haye Sainte. His preliminary bombardment from eighty cannons largely missed the British hidden behind the slope. As the French reached the hedge-lined road, the British popped up and

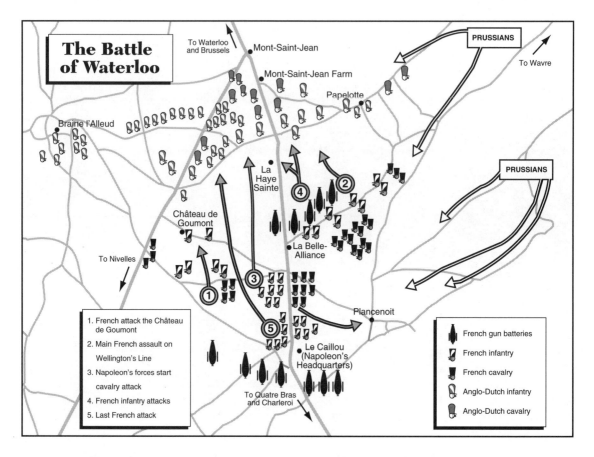

The Battle of Waterloo

PRUSSIANS

To Waterloo and Brussels

Mont-Saint-Jean

To Wavre

Mont-Saint-Jean Farm

Papelotte

Braine l'Alleud

PRUSSIANS

La Haye Sainte

④

②

Château de Goumont

La Belle-Alliance

To Nivelles

③

Plancenoit

①

⑤

Le Caillou (Napoleon's Headquarters)

1. French attack the Château de Goumont
2. Main French assault on Wellington's Line
3. Napoleon's forces start cavalry attack
4. French infantry attacks
5. Last French attack

French gun batteries

French infantry

French cavalry

Anglo-Dutch infantry

Anglo-Dutch cavalry

To Quatre Bras and Charleroi

blasted them with musket fire and then sent in a cavalry counterattack that threw the French back. Finally, as new French bombardments began to destroy the center of the British defenses, Marshal Ney impulsively decided to send his cavalry in to finish the job. Unfortunately, the British were ready. As a veteran would later recall,

[the French cavalry's] pace was a slow but steady trot. None of your furious galloping charges was this, but a deliberate advance, at a deliberate pace, as of men resolved to carry their point. . . . The only sound that could be heard from them amidst the incessant roar of battle was the low thunder-like reverberation of the ground beneath the simul-

taneous tread of so many horses. On our part was equal deliberation. Every man stood quietly by his post, the guns ready, loaded with a round-shot first and a case over it. . . . The port fires glared and sputtered behind the wheels; and my word alone was wanting [needed] to hurl destruction on that goodly show of gallant men and noble horses.[102]

By 6:00 P.M., Napoleon was faced with a desperate situation. Ney had finally taken La Haye Sainte, but Wellington's overall position was holding and Blücher's forces had arrived and were starting to attack the French rear. Ney, mad with the fury of battle, began feeding Napoleon's precious Imperial Guard into the assault on the center of the British line, which rose to a climax of cannon and musket fire. A British soldier later reported that

suddenly the firing ceased, and as the smoke cleared away a superb sight opened on us. A close column of Grenadiers (about seventy in front) . . . were seen ascending the rise. . . . They continued to advance till within fifty or sixty paces of our front, when the [British] brigade was ordered to stand up. Whether it was from the sudden and unexpected appearance of a Corps so near them, which must have seemed as starting [springing] out of the ground, or the tremendous heavy fire we threw into them, *La Garde*, which had never before failed in an attack, *suddenly* stopped.[103]

French Bravery at Waterloo

In this quote from Philip J. Haythornthwaite's The Napoleonic Sourcebook, *Edward Creasey gives an example of astonishing bravery and fortitude by French soldiers.*

"Never, indeed, had the national bravery of the French people been more nobly shown. One soldier in the French ranks was seen, when his arm was shattered by a cannon-ball, to wrench it off with the other; and throwing it up in the air, he exclaimed to his comrades, 'Vive l'Empereur jusqu' à la mort' [Long live the Emperor, until death!]. . . . At the beginning of the action, a French soldier who had both legs carried off by a cannon-ball, was borne past the front of Foy's division, and called out to them, ['It's nothing, comrades; Long live the Emperor, Glory to France!']

The same officer, at the end of the battle, when all hope was lost, tells us that he saw a French grenadier, blackened with powder, and with his clothes torn and stained, leaning on his musket, and immovable as a statue. The colonel called to him to join his comrades and retreat; but the grenadier showed him his musket and his hands, and said 'These hands have with this musket used to-day more than twenty packets of cartridges: it was more than my share: I supplied myself with ammunition from the dead. Leave me to die here on the field of battle. It is not courage that fails me, but strength.'"

Napoleon watches as his troops fall to the British at Waterloo. The defeat ended both Napoleon's career and France's expansionist endeavors.

Both the battle and Napoleon's career were over. Ever since the battle's end, historians have debated whether Napoleon might have won if Grouchy had properly blocked the defeated Prussians, if the attack of the Imperial Guard had been coordinated rather than piecemeal, or if Napoleon had realized that Ney had lost all sense of judgment. But even if Napoleon had won at Waterloo, the allies would still have had overwhelming forces and resources. While a victorious Napoleon might have been allowed to rule a France with its more modest, original boundaries, it is doubtful that Napoleon, being Napoleon, would have been satisfied to be just one ruler among many.

Epilogue

Napoleon's Legacy and the Modern World

Following his defeat at Waterloo, Napoleon cast about for a means of escape. He considered sailing to America, which might have caused considerable problems for the young United States. However, British vigilance and a lack of willing accomplices quickly led to Napoleon's arrest and deportation to the remote island of St. Helena, where he lived out his years, writing his memoirs before dying on May 5, 1821, at the age of fifty-one, the victim of ulcers, stomach cancer, poison, or some combination of these misfortunes.

In the aftermath of Napoleon, the leaders at the Congress of Vienna tried to put the old monarchies of Europe back together. To some extent they succeeded, but the French revolution's ideas of "liberty, equality, and fraternity" could not easily be suppressed. The industrialization, workers' struggles, and revolts that led to 1848, known as "the Year of Revolutions," taught leaders that they had to pay attention to the popular will. At the same time, nationalism encouraged the formation of large, powerful states.

As one historian puts it:

Napoleon solved a crucial problem of national size. His conquests created states that were of the right acreage to become modern nation-states. Places like Corsica and the German principalities were too small to survive; all Europe, as he found out, expensively, was too big to rule. But states the size of Napoleonic France and post-Napoleonic Germany were just right.[104]

Large states, plus the coming technology of railroads, steel ships, and breech-loading cannon, would mean that the destructiveness of war would outstrip even the greatest imaginings of Napoleon or Wellington.

Napoleon was always keenly concerned with what history would have to say about him:

For all the attempts to restrict, suppress and muffle me, it will be difficult to make me disappear from the public memory completely. French historians will have to deal with the Empire . . . and will have to give me my rightful due.

Ah, no doubt [the historian] will find that I had ambition, a great deal of it— but the grandest and noblest, perhaps, that ever was: the ambition of establishing and consecrating at last

Napoleon and Hitler

In Napoleon and Hitler: A Comparative Biography, *Desmond Seward describes Napoleon's personality and points out that the German dictator shared some of the same traits. He does not, however, suggest that if Napoleon had continued in power he would have foreshadowed Hitler by systematically killing millions of civilian men, women, and children.*

"The reason why Napoleon would never even contemplate any form of peace is that he believed that surrendering territory would weaken his authority over his people, diminishing that absolute power which he loved above all else. He was a gambler on a gigantic scale. When he had lost his empire he still hoped to keep his country for himself, either by a single brilliant feat of arms or through some political miracle. The sufferings of his people, let alone those of conquered races, did not enter his mind.

Exactly the same considerations explain the Führer's [Hitler's] behavior in similar circumstances. He too was an absolutist, whose stakes were all or nothing, tortured by his obscene love of power. And he too lacked any compassion whatever for his fellow-men, to an even more terrible degree."

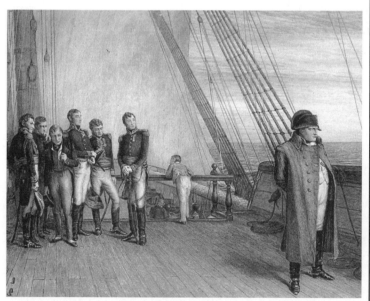

A prisoner of war, Napoleon stands dejectedly aboard a British ship after his surrender.

During the Age of Napoleon, French society, military, and government were transformed. Napoleon, the enterprising figure who lent his name to the era, stood at the forefront of these changes.

the kingdom of reason and the full exercise, the complete enjoyment, of all human capabilities! And in this respect the historian will perhaps find himself forced to regret that such an ambition has not been fulfilled.[105]

As one author insightfully noted, "For the French, Napoleon is not just an icon; he is a constellation, high in the sky, and no more to be judged good or evil than the stars are." The same author goes on to point out, however, that "in his own time, and for most of the nineteenth century, his career was irresistably projected backward as a retelling of Alexander the Great's. In our time, it is hard not to project it forward as a first draft of Hitler's."[106]

That very difference in perceptions reveals the historical changes that began in the Age of Napoleon. The French Revolution had asserted liberty and promised democracy, equal treatment, and reward for merit. At the same time, the destruction of the intricate local structure of feudalism and its replacement with powerful central governments made it possible for ruthless leaders to use propaganda and the machinery of the police state to wage war or terror on an unprecedented scale. In many ways Napoleon pioneered the kind of dictatorship that Hitler and Stalin would bring to terrifying perfection in the twentieth century.

Ironically, two world wars would lead many modern people to look back on the Age of Napoleon with a kind of nostalgia. Hobbyists would paint detailed miniatures of the soldiers of the many armies of the time in their colorful uniforms. War-game enthusiasts would refight Austerlitz and Waterloo with cardboard markers and, later, on personal computers. General, emperor, and supreme gambler, Napoleon continues to fascinate generations of historians and storytellers.

Notes

Introduction: The Birth of the Modern

1. Leo Tolstoy, *War and Peace*. London: BCA, 1971, p. 888.

Chapter 1: Seizing the Day: Napoleon's Revolutionary Opportunity

2. Quoted in Will and Ariel Durant, *The Age of Napoleon: A History of European Civilization from 1789 to 1815*. New York: Simon & Schuster, 1975, p. 5.

3. Quoted in J. Christopher Herold, *The Age of Napoleon*. New York: American Heritage, 1963, p. 31.

4. Quoted in David G. Chandler, *On the Napoleonic Wars*. Mechanicsburg, PA: Stackpole Books, 1994, p. 49.

5. Quoted in Chandler, *On the Napoleonic Wars*, p. 48.

6. Quoted in James Harvey Robinson, *Readings in European History*. Boston: Ginn, 1906, p. 456.

7. Quoted in Herold, *The Age of Napoleon*, p. 46.

8. Quoted in Durant, *The Age of Napoleon*, p. 63.

9. Quoted in Durant, *The Age of Napoleon*, p. 91.

10. Alan Schom, *Napoleon Bonaparte*. New York: HarperCollins, 1997, p. 5.

11. Quoted in Schom, *Napoleon Bonaparte*, p. 7.

12. Quoted in Schom, *Napoleon Bonaparte*, p. 11.

13. Quoted in Herold, *The Age of Napoleon*, pp. 8–9.

14. Quoted in Alan Schom, *Napoleon Bonaparte*, 1997, p. 22.

Chapter 2: Learning His Craft: Napoleon in Italy and Egypt

15. Herold, *The Age of Napoleon*, p. 52.

16. Quoted in Albert Sidney Britt III, *The Wars of Napoleon*. West Point Military History Series. Wayne, NJ: Avery, 1985, p. 6.

17. Quoted in Schom, *Napoleon Bonaparte*, p. 45.

18. Durant, *The Age of Napoleon*, pp. 98–99.

19. Quoted in Herold, *The Age of Napoleon*, p. 46.

20. Quoted in Philip J. Haythornthwaite et al., *Napoleon: The Final Verdict*. London: Arms and Armour, 1996, p. 34.

21. Quoted in Schom, *Napoleon Bonaparte*, p. 47.

22. Quoted in Durant, pp. 48–49.

23. Quoted in Adam Gopnik, "The Good Soldier," *The New Yorker*, November 24, 1997, p. 109.

24. Britt, *The Wars of Napoleon*, p. 13.

25. Quoted in Britt, *The Wars of Napoleon*, p. 19.

26. Quoted in Schom, *Napoleon Bonaparte*, p. 66.

27. Quoted in *Translations and Reprints from the Original Sources of European History*. Vol. II, no. 2. Philadelphia: University of Pennsylvania Press, 1897–1907, p. 2.

28. Michael Rapport, "Napoleon's Rise to Power," *History Today*, vol. 48, no. 1, January 1998, p. 12.

29. Quoted in Schom, *Napoleon Bonaparte*, p. 89.

30. Schom, *Napoleon Bonaparte*, p. 115.

31. Quoted in Durant, *The Age of Napoleon*, p. 109.

32. Quoted in Schom, *Napoleon Bonaparte*, p. 111.

33. Quoted in Schom, *Napoleon Bonaparte*, pp. 119–20.

34. Quoted in Durant, *The Age of Napoleon*, p. 110.

35. Mahmoud Hussein, "The Eagle and the Sphinx: Bonaparte in Egypt," *UNESCO Courier*, June 1989, p. 24.

Chapter 3: Transforming the Republic: Napoleon Remakes France

36. Quoted in Schom, *Napoleon Bonaparte*, p. 189.

37. Quoted in Hippolyte Taine, *The French Revolution*. Vol. 3. New York: Henry Holt, 1891, p. 467n.

38. Quoted in Durant, *The Age of Napoleon*, p. 120.

39. Quoted in Durant, *The Age of Napoleon*, p. 122.

40. Quoted in Haythornthwaite, *Napoleon: The Final Verdict*, 1996, p. 39.

41. Quoted in Herold, *The Age of Napoleon*, p. 94.

42. Quoted in Herold, *The Age of Napoleon*, p. 148–149.

43. Quoted in Haythornthwaite, *Napoleon: The Final Verdict*, p. 41.

44. Quoted in Durant, *The Age of Napoleon*, p. 180.

45. Quoted in Douglas Hilt, *Ten Against Napoleon*. Chicago: Nelson Hall, 1975, p. 164.

46. Quoted in Herold, *The Age of Napoleon*, pp. 165–66.

47. Quoted in Schom, *Napoleon Bonaparte*, pp. 262–63.

48. Quoted in Bob Carroll, *Napoleon Bonaparte*. San Diego: Lucent Books, 1994, p. 11.

Chapter 4: Marching to Empire: Napoleon, Britain, and the German States

49. Quoted in Durant, *The Age of Napoleon*, p. 179.

50. Quoted in Charles J. Esdaile, *The Wars of Napoleon*. New York: Longman, 1995, p. 158.

51. Quoted in Esdaile, *The Wars of Napoleon*, p. 159.

52. Quoted in Chandler, *On the Napoleonic Wars*, pp. 49–50.

53. Quoted in Alan Schom, *One Hundred Days*. New York: Atheneum; Maxwell Macmillan International, 1992, p. 273.

54. Quoted in Schom, *Napoleon Bonaparte*, p. 329.

55. Quoted in Alan Schom, *Trafalgar: Countdown to Battle, 1803–1805*. New York: Atheneum, 1990, pp. 59-62.

56. Quoted in Schom, *Napoleon Bonaparte*, p. 362.

57. Herold, *The Age of Napoleon*, p. 242.

58. John Prados, "Napoleon Bonaparte," in *The Reader's Companion to Military History*, eds. Robert Cowley and Geoffrey Parker. Boston: Houghton Mifflin, 1996, p. 320.

59. Haythornthwaite, *Napoleon: The Final Verdict*, p. 217.

60. Geoffrey Ellis, *The Napoleonic Empire*. London: Macmillan, 1991, p. 58.

61. Quoted in Britt, *The Wars of Napoleon*, p. 45.

62. Quoted in Segur, *An Aide de Camp to Napoleon*. Trans. H. A. Patchett-Martin. New York: D. Appleton, 1895, p. 238.

63. Quoted in Schom, *Napoleon Bonaparte*, p. 417–18.

64. Michael Broers, "The Empire Behind the Lines," *History Today*, vol. 48, no. 1, January 1998, p. 20.

65. Quoted in Carroll, *Napoleon Bonaparte*, p. 90.

66. Quoted in Carroll, *Napoleon Bonaparte*, p. 90.

Chapter 5: Changing the Rules: Unconventional War in Spain and Russia

67. Rafael Altamira, *A History of Spain*. Princeton, NJ: Van Nostrand, 1949, p. 536.

68. Herold, *Age of Napoleon*, p. 210.

69. Quoted in Britt, *The Wars of Napoleon*, p. 84.

70. Quoted in Britt, *The Wars of Napoleon*, p. 85.

71. Quoted in Schom, *Napoleon Bonaparte*, p. 471.

72. Quoted in Britt, *The Wars of Napoleon*, p. 88.

73. Herold, *The Age of Napoleon*, p. 217.

74. Quoted in Esdaile, *The Wars of Napoleon*, p. 130.

75. Quoted in W. Hargreaves-Mawdseley, ed., *Spain under the Bourbons, 1700–1833*. Vol. I. London: Macmillan, 1973, p. 223.

76. H. von Brandt, *The Two Minas and the Spanish Guerrillas.* London, 1825, pp. 56–58.

77. J. Walter, *The Diary of a Napoleonic Foot Soldier.* Ed., M. Raeff. New York: Doubleday, 1991, pp. 24–25.

78. Quoted in Haythornthwaite, *Napoleon: The Final Verdict,* pp. 108–109.

79. Quoted in Esdaile, *The Wars of Napoleon,* p. 221.

80. Quoted in Britt, *The Wars of Napoleon,* p. 106.

81. Quoted in Britt, *The Wars of Napoleon,* p. 110.

82. Schom, *Napoleon Bonaparte,* pp. 594–95.

83. Quoted in Antony Brett-James, *1812: Eyewitness Accounts of Napoleon's Defeat in Russia.* New York: St. Martin's Press, 1966, p. 54.

84. Quoted in Schom, *Napoleon Bonaparte,* p. 602.

85. Quoted in Chandler, *The Napoleonic Wars,* pp. 186–87.

86. Quoted in Herold, *The Age of Napoleon,* p. 7.

87. Quoted in Schom, *Napoleon Bonaparte,* p. 636.

88. Quoted in Chandler, *The Napoleonic Wars,* pp. 186–87.

89. Quoted in Haythornthwaite, *Napoleon: The Final Verdict,* p. 132.

Chapter 6: Defeating Napoleon: The European War of Liberation

90. Quoted in Markham, *Napoleon,* p. 188.

91. Quoted in Britt, *The Wars of Napoleon,* p. 106.

92. Quoted in Britt, *The Wars of Napoleon,* p. 92.

93. Paul Johnson, *The Birth of the Modern: World Society, 1815–1830.* New York: HarperCollins, 1991, p. 98.

94. Quoted in Herold, *The Age of Napoleon,* p. 406.

95. Quoted in Schom, *Napoleon Bonaparte,* p. 708.

96. Schom, *Napoleon Bonaparte,* pp. 712–13.

97. Quoted in Schom, *Napoleon Bonaparte,* p. 721.

98. Quoted in Schom, *Napoleon Bonaparte,* pp. 720–21.

99. Quoted in Haythornthwaite, *Napoleon: The Final Verdict,* p. 174.

100. Quoted in Haythornthwaite, *Napoleon: The Final Verdict,* p. 174.

101. Quoted in Christopher Hibbert, *Wellington: A Personal History.* Reading, MA: Addison-Wesley, 1997, p. 178.

102. Cavalie Mercer, *Journal of the Waterloo Campaign.* New York: Praeger, 1969, p. 174.

103. Quoted in Britt, *The Wars of Napoleon,* p. 161.

Epilogue: Napoleon's Legacy and the Modern World

104. Gopnik, "The Good Soldier," p. 114.

105. Quoted in Herold, *The Age of Napoleon,* p. 431.

106. Gopnik, "The Good Soldier," p. 106.

For Further Reading

Bob Carroll, *Napoleon Bonaparte*. San Diego: Lucent Books, 1994. Lively biography of Napoleon for young people in Lucent's The Importance Of series.

David C. Chandler, *The Illustrated Napoleon*. New York: Henry Holt, 1990. Extensively illustrated with drawings, paintings, maps, battle plans, and other materials.

J. Christopher Herold, *The Age of Napoleon*. Boston: Houghton Mifflin, 1963. One of the most readable overviews of Napoleon's life and the struggle for Europe.

Albert Marrin, *Napoleon and the Napoleonic Wars*. New York: Viking, 1991. Vivid, detailed account of Napoleon's life and battles, suitable for junior high and high school readers.

Major Works Consulted

Brent Bosworthy, *With Musket, Cannon, and Sword: Battle Tactics of Napoleon and His Enemies.* New York: Sarpedon, 1996. Detailed discussion of the development of training and tactics during the Napoleonic Wars.

Albert Sidney Britt III, *The Wars of Napoleon.* Wayne, NJ: Avery, 1985. Part of the West Point Military History Series, this book offers a detailed discussion of the background and tactics for each of Napoleon's campaigns.

Gregor Dallas, *The Final Act: The Roads to Waterloo.* New York: Henry Holt, 1996. Vivid depiction of the climactic years of 1814 and 1815, when European leaders struggled to contain Napoleon while forging a new political order.

Will and Ariel Durant, *The Age of Napoleon: A History of European Civilization from 1789 to 1815.* New York: Simon & Schuster, 1975. A volume in the Durants' classic history of civilization and quite readable despite its size and scope. Gives a systematic view of Napoleon's life, the administration of the French Empire, developments in England and other countries, and a comprehensive look at literature, the arts, scientific developments, and philosophy of the period.

Charles J. Esdaile, *The Wars of Napoleon.* New York: Longman, 1995. Combines military history (with its focus on campaigns and battles) and the study of the political, social, and economic background of the conflict. The result is a clear evaluation of the factors that contributed to Napoleon's success and his eventual downfall as well as the impact of the Napoleonic Wars on the shaping of the nineteenth century.

Philip J. Haythornthwaite, et al., *Napoleon: The Final Verdict.* London: Arms and Armour Press, 1996. A collection of essays that evaluate Napoleon's effectiveness as a commander, planner, and strategist. Each essay focuses on a particular part of Napoleon's career and campaigns.

Christopher Hibbert, *Wellington: A Personal History.* Reading, MA: Addison-Wesley, 1997. Detailed biography of the second most interesting commander in the Napoleonic Wars.

Paul Johnson, *The Birth of the Modern: World Society, 1815–1830.* New York: Harper-Collins, 1991. A massive but readable look at the many ways in which the world was changing during the years immediately following the end of the Napoleonic Wars. Discusses events, culture, social history, and technology.

George F. Nafziger, *Napoleon's Invasion of Russia.* Novato, CA: Presidio Press, 1988. Good account of Napoleon's most ambitious campaign.

Alan Schom, *Napoleon Bonaparte.* New York: HarperCollins, 1997. An extensive biography of Napoleon reflecting recent scholarship.

Additional Works Consulted

Rafael Altamira, *A History of Spain.* Princeton, NJ: Van Nostand, 1949.

E. A. Arnold, ed. and trans., *A Documentary Survey of Napoleonic France.* Lanham, MD: University Press of America, 1994.

John W. Barrett, *European History, 1789 to 1848: Revolution and the New European Order.* Piscataway, NJ: Research and Education Association, 1996.

John Belchem and Richard Price, eds., *The Penguin Dictionary of Nineteenth-Century History.* New York: Penguin Books, 1996.

Louis Bergeron, *France Under Napoleon.* Trans. R. R. Palmer. Princeton, NJ: Princeton University Press, 1981.

Olivier Bernier, *Words of Fire, Deeds of Blood: The Mob, the Monarchy, and the French Revolution.* Boston: Little, Brown, 1989.

Jeremy Black, "Napoleon's Impact on International Relations," *History Today,* vol. 48, no. 2, February 1998.

Jeremy Black and Roy Porter, eds, *The Penguin Dictionary of Eighteenth-Century History.* New York: Penguin Books, 1996.

H. von Brandt, *The Two Minas and the Spanish Guerrillas.* London, 1825.

Antony Brett-James, *1812: Eyewitness Accounts of Napoleon's Defeat in Russia.* New York: St. Martin's Press, 1966.

Michael Broers, "The Empire Behind the Lines," *History Today,* vol.48, no. 1, January 1998.

Somerset de Chair, ed., *Napoleon on Napoleon: An Autobiography of the Emperor.* London: Cassell, 1992.

David G. Chandler, *Atlas of Military Strategy: The Art, Theory, and Practice of War, 1618–1878.* London: Arms and Armour Press, 1980.

David G. Chandler, *On the Napoleonic Wars.* Mechanicsburg, PA: Stackpole Books, 1994.

David G. Chandler, *Waterloo: The Hundred Days.* New York: Macmillan, 1981.

Robert Cowley and Geoffrey Parker, eds., *The Reader's Companion to Military History.* Boston: Houghton Mifflin, 1996.

George C. D'Aguilar, *The Military Maxims of Napoleon.* New York: Da Capo Press, 1995.

H. T. Dickinson, ed., *Britain and the French Revolution, 1789–1815.* Basingstoke, England: Macmillan, 1989.

Geoffrey Ellis, *The Napoleonic Empire.* London: Macmillan, 1991.

Clive Emsley, *The Longman Companion to Napoleonic Europe.* New York: Longman, 1993.

David Gates, *The Spanish Ulcer.* New York: Norton, 1986.

Adam Gopnik, "The Good Soldier," *The New Yorker,* November 24, 1997.

A. D. Harvey, "Napoleon—The Myth," *History Today,* vol. 48, no. 1, January 1998.

Philip J. Haythornthwaite, *Die Hard! Dramatic Actions from the Napoleonic Wars.* New York: Arms and Armour Press, 1996.

Philip J. Haythornthwaite, *The Napoleonic Sourcebook.* New York: Facts On File, 1990.

J. Christopher Herold, *The Mind of Napoleon: A Selection from His Written and Spoken Words.* New York: Columbia University Press, 1995.

Douglas Hilt, *Ten Against Napoleon.* Chicago: Nelson Hall, 1975.

Mahmoud Hussein, "The Eagle and the Sphinx: Bonaparte in Egypt," *UNESCO Courier,* June 1989.

Caralie Mercer, *Journal of the Waterloo Campaign.* New York: Praeger, 1969.

Michael Rapport, "Napoleon's Rise to Power," *History Today,* vol. 48, no. 1, January 1998.

James Harvey Robinson, *Readings in European History.* Boston: Ginn, 1906.

George Rudé, *Revolutionary Europe, 1783–1815.* New York: Harper & Row, 1964.

Alan Schom, *One Hundred Days.* New York: Atheneum; Maxwell Macmillan International, 1992.

Alan Schom, *Trafalgar: Countdown to Battle, 1803–1805.* New York: Atheneum, 1990.

Sequr, *An Aide de Camp to Napoleon.* Trans. H. A. Patchett-Martin. New York: D. Appleton, 1895.

Desmond Seward, *Napoleon and Hitler: A Comparative Biography.* New York: Viking Penguin, 1989.

Hippolyte Taine, *The French Revolution.* Vol. 3. New York: Henry Holt, 1891.

A. J. P. Taylor, *From Napoleon to the Second International: Essays on Nineteenth-Century Europe.* New York: Penguin Books, 1995.

A. W. Thayer, *Life of Ludwig von Beethoven.* Vol. II. Princeton, NJ: Princeton University Press, 1964.

Leo Tolstoy, *War and Peace.* London: BCA, 1971.

William T. Walker, *The Essentials of European History: 1848 to 1914: Realism and Materialism.* Piscataway, NJ: Research and Education Association, 1990.

Bruce Waller, ed., *Themes in Modern European History.* New York: Routledge, 1992.

J. Walter, *The Diary of a Napoleonic Foot Soldier.* Ed. M. Raeff. New York: Doubleday, 1991.

Eugen Weber, *Europe Since 1715: A Modern History.* New York: W. W. Norton, 1972.

Esmond Wright, ed., *An Illustrated History of the Modern World.* New York: McGraw-Hill, 1964.

Index

Picture Credits

About the Author

Harry Henderson has written a number of books about computers and the Internet, science, and biography. His titles for Lucent include *The Scientific Revolution* and *Twentieth Century Science* (both coauthored with his wife, Lisa Yount), *The Importance of Stephen Hawking*, and *The Internet*. He lives in El Cerrito, California, with his wife, four cats, and thousands of books.